101 Medieval Churches of East Sussex

A TOURING GUIDE

PAUL COPPIN

ILLUSTRATIONS BY THE AUTHOR

S.B. Publications

This book is dedicated to my wife Janice, without whom
I would have accomplished very little
in the last thirty years, let alone this book.

ACKNOWLEDGEMENTS

My thanks go to all the vicars, rectors and churchwardens who were only too pleased to show me round their churches, especially those at Burwash, Etchingham and South Malling.

My very special thanks go to John Martin, who assisted me with the research and accompanied me on some very long fact-finding tours; and my wife for her help in correcting and compiling the finished book.

First published in 2001 by S B Publications
19 Grove Road, Seaford, Sussex BN25 1TP
01323 893498
fax 01323 893860
sales@sbpublications.swinternet.co.uk

© Paul Coppin 2001
The moral right of the author has been asserted

ISBN 1 85770 238 7

Typeset by JEM Editorial (JEMedit@AOL.com)
Printed by Tansleys the Printers
19 Broad Street
Seaford
Sussex BN25 1LS
01323 891019

CONTENTS

Front Cover: Laughton Church
Back Cover: Friston Church

INTRODUCTION

hree years ago, after buying a small weekend retreat in Sussex, I decided to combine three of my interests — medieval history, photography and car touring — and visit all the ancient village churches in East Sussex. I thought this would be a pleasurable way to learn more about an area that has seen so much of England's early history, and so it has proved to be. I soon found that, although there were some good guide books, there were none that had pictures of all the churches, gave directions to them or even rated the churches in the simplest of ways. So, almost from the start, this book took shape.

I have kept to the ancient village churches because they are the ones that have evolved with the county, often playing a major role in their particular areas for more than 1,000 years, and although they have changed over the years, they all retain something of their simple beginnings. It is true there are some superb town churches, but rapid population growth in the last 200 years has had a much greater and more sudden effect on them, and they are very different from the village churches. The exceptions are in Rye, Hastings, Battle, Bexhill, Lewes, Newhaven, Seaford and Eastbourne, all of which (except Lewes) are in their respective 'old towns' and both church and area have retained a village persona. With these eight exceptions, there are in this book no churches in major towns and none that do not contain at least a major feature built prior to 1800. No two churches are the same, and every church, without exception, contains something of interest.

It was suggested that I give each church a rating of some kind, and initially I was not happy with this idea as all rating systems must reflect the writer's view, at least to some extent. In the end it seemed best to rate them according to what they actually possess in three categories — architectural features, settings, historic interest. In all three areas, East Sussex churches excel. In some churches a thousand years of architectural change can be seen, and as for the settings, some of these are the best in England — although we may have our pagan ancestors to thank for that. They chose particularly attractive natural sites for their holy places, and early Christians built their churches on the same sites.

Throughout the book are sections on the various areas of the church and its grounds. These are intended to assist the reader in how to look at a church to get the most from it. The uninitiated often rush straight to the door and miss perhaps 60 per cent of the features by so doing. The secret is to take it slowly and look in all the corners, inside and out, up and down.

I am often asked about gaining access to churches, and it is true that theft and vandalism have caused more churches to be locked, but East Sussex fares better than most counties. Perhaps three in ten are locked during the week, but at least one of these three will have details of where the key is kept. Once inside, always sign the visitors' book; this is often used as a guide for whether to keep the church open. Remember, too, that the upkeep of even the smallest village church is well over £100 a week, with some costing as much as £200 a day to run, so think about buying a guide book or a postcard, or just dropping a few coins in the collection box.

During the writing of this book I have visited all the churches at least twice, taken more than 500 photographs, driven 1,000 miles and grown to love the county and its churches more every week — so much so that I have now sold the weekend place and moved home from London to Lewes. If readers get a fraction of the enjoyment from this book that I have had in writing it, then it will have been worth producing. Now it's finished I'm going to miss my weekend church crawls — but there's always West Sussex.

Paul Coppin

HOW TO USE THIS BOOK

Churches are grouped together in areas, and their locations are indicated by the page number of the East Sussex Ordnance Survey Street Atlas (OSSA). Church ratings are in three categories: 🏛 interesting architectural or building features; ❀ picturesque settings or views; ✩ historical or unusual interest. Ratings are from none to three of each. On page 140 there is a plan of a typical medieval church.

CHURCH DEDICATIONS

here is a lot more to ancient church dedications than might at first be considered. They fall into three types, those linked with various Christian cults that were in vogue between the tenth and fourteenth centuries, those linked with particular people, places or pilgrimages, and those of a general nature.

The church visitor often ignores the dedication, which is a mistake as it can often tell us much about the church itself. For example, churches dedicated to St Michael usually fall into the first group, being most often linked to a widespread Christian cult whose members favoured this saint. Almost always, churches bearing St Michael's name are built on high ground, as are those named after St Catherine. Churches dedicated to St Anne are usually close to a well or stream (although the cult following this saint was not strong as far south as Sussex and there is now only one dedication to St Anne in East Sussex, that being in Lewes). The cult of St George arrived in England with the returning crusaders and it was at that time that this saint replaced St Edward the Confessor as England's patron saint. St George is well represented, however, with six. Those churches dedicated to St George were, for the most part, built after the crusades. These cults favouring a particular saint could be quite localised. St Giles is a good example, West Sussex has a large number of churches named after this saint whereas East Sussex has only two.

St Dunstan's at Mayfield falls into the second group. Dunstan, during the time he was a bishop, built churches on all his estates, including that at Mayfield. After his canonisation this church was rebuilt and dedicated to him.

St Thomas à Becket had links with East Sussex and, after his death, three churches in the county had their dedications changed to honour him.

The third group is by far the largest. The most popular dedication is to St Mary, there being twenty-four in Sussex, followed by St Peter with sixteen and All Saints with thirteen. Even these general dedications have something to say. The top two in the popularity chart remind us that all these parish churches were originally under the influence of the Church of Rome.

Being a strong Saxon area Sussex has its share of Saxon saints like St Wulfran (Ovingdean), one of only two in England, and St Oswald (Hooe). The dedication to All Saints is also often indicative of Saxon origins so its strong presence is not surprising. There are some very rare and unusual dedications to be found. At Keymer the church is one of only three in the country dedicated to two North African brothers St Cosmas and St Damian, the patron saints of pharmacy and medicine , who were martyred in the fourth century. At Buxted another somewhat obscure saint is honoured, here the church is dedicated to St Margaret, Queen of the Scots.

Some churches have no dedication although they surely must have had as the feast day of a church's patron saint played an important part in the early days of Christianity in England, as a bridge between pagan rites and Christian festivals. Evidence of lost dedications can be seen at East Chiltington where the building started life as a church, became a chapel, when it probably lost its dedication, then became a church again with its patron saint forgotten; and at Lullington where the church was destroyed and lay in ruins for centuries before its restoration. Here there is some clue to the dedication in an old bequest which makes mention of 'a taper to be set before St Sithe in the church of the same'.

OVINGDEAN *St Wulfran* OSSA 164 🏛 🏛 🍁 ☆

Almost all of this beautiful downland church was built between 1100 and 1200, with only the south chapel being a recent addition. Most of the windows are lancets, some in the tower and nave being very narrow. The original Norman doorway in the north wall (now blocked) is very clear both inside and out and the holy water stoup can still be seen next to it.

A great rarity is the fourteenth century rood screen which somehow survived and is now positioned behind the altar. The chancel arch and blocked high round window are of the same date as the north door.

There was a south aisle, the arches of which can still be seen in the present south wall. This aisle may have been destroyed by fire as the stones of the arches show some signs of flame damage. This area was a popular landing place for French raiders in the thirteenth century, and they certainly set fire to Rottingdean church just a mile or so to the south, so perhaps Ovingdean suffered the same fate.

The original small churchyard is very crowded and has now been enlarged to the west; the very large tomb is for the Kempe family and was designed by the artist Charles Kempe who also designed most of the stained glass and the rood.

The church dedication to St Wulfran is almost unique with only one other in England (at Grantham, Lincolnshire). How this Saxon saint, active in the north of England, came to have a church dedicated to him on the south coast we will probably never know.

ROTTINGDEAN *St Margaret* OSSA 167 🏛 🍁 ☆☆

There was certainly a church here in Saxon times but if anything from that building remains it could only be a few stones in the north wall. The early Norman south wall was lost when the aisle was added, but most of the north wall is eleventh century. Unusually, the early church had a tower, almost certainly built for defence, but it collapsed within 100 years and the present very sturdy and heavily buttressed tower was built in 1205. This later tower also had a defensive use, during the 100 Years War in the thirteenth century. French raiders set fire to the tower, killing all those who had taken refuge there; the cracked stones are visible from inside the tower.

The stained glass in the north nave and east windows were designed by Edward Burne-Jones, the pre-Raphaelite artist, and were made by William Morris. Burne-Jones lived in the village and a memorial to him can be found in the church wall a little south of the west door. The large carved chair in the chancel was given by former Prime Minister Stanley Baldwin and his wife on the fiftieth anniversary of their marriage in the church.

There are many interesting memorials inside the church but perhaps the most interesting is the bust of Dr Hooker, a former vicar generally regarded as the 'lookout man' for the local smugglers — and even today he seems to be doing just that from his perch high above the pulpit.

The churchyard contains some old stones and two (restored) wooden grave boards. A little searching will reveal the grave of a popular music hall star, GH Elliott, whose stage name was 'the Chocolate-coloured Coon'.

TELSCOMBE *St Laurence* OSSA 167 🍁 ☆☆

he road leading to Telscombe must offer some of the best views of the South Downs, running as it does along the top of a ridge before dropping into the wooded hollow containing the village.

The church, which sits up high above the village, is almost all twelfth century with the Sussex capped tower and north chapel being added a little later. The nave arcade has simple Norman pillars supporting round arches of the early Norman period. On one of the pillars two crusader crosses can be seen, believed to have been carved by men keeping vigil before going to the crusades. The Lady chapel was restored by the Thornton-Smith family in 1937 and contains an altar brought from Verona and a modern window containing dozens of fragments of fourteenth century glass brought from the north of England. A late twelfth century lancet in the west wall contains interesting early glass depicting a dove and a Pelican piercing its own heart symbolising the holy spirit and the sacrifice of the cross.

The wooded well-populated churchyard climbs away up the considerable slope the church is built on and contains some large old stones.

PATCHAM *All Saints* OSSA 142   🏛 ⭐⭐

The first reaction upon reaching Patcham church might well be one of disappointment for it is not a pretty thing. The whole of the west, south and east sides have been faced with cement. You may feel like turning away, and that would be a mistake. The church is old, possibly very old in places. The odd remaining corbel suggests that the outside was in a very poor state and hence the cement which, if nothing else, gives an impression of what churches looked like in Medieval times when most were rendered.

From the outside the only clues to the age are the Decorated style windows in the nave and chancel (fourteenth century) and the older lancets in the tower (thirteenth). Inside the church's age becomes clearer. The chancel arch is late twelfth century and the door in the north wall, which has been moved from some other part of the building, could be Saxon. The tie beams in the queen post roof are of great age.

The Doom painting above the chancel arch, uncovered during Victorian restoration, dates from the thirteenth century and is thought to be the oldest in the country. There is a full set of commandment and prayer boards on the west wall; these were mandatory in churches at one time, and many have survived in Sussex.

In the churchyard is an area of five or six chest tombs, which are almost identical to each other and seem to be for members of the same family. To the north is a memorial for a smuggler 'unfortunately shot', evidence of the common practice of using only the north side of a churchyard for suicides and criminals.

LEWES (CLIFFE)
St Thomas à Becket
OSSA 123 ☆

Although the town of Lewes has absorbed the village of Cliffe, it still maintains its own personality, this being due in no small way to the presence of the church at the end of the High Street.

Originally a twelfth century chapel of ease attached to the Benedictine college at South Malling, it was enlarged in the fourteenth century and the tower was added in the fifteenth century. Remaining today from Norman times are the nave pillars, the north west end of the aisle and most of the chancel.

Between 1576 and 1690 the living was in the gift of the Archbishop of Canterbury, after that date it moved to the Crown which still holds it today.

In the tower are a copy of the Cliffe Charter complete with the great seal of Henry IV and a charity trust board dated 1603. This trust is still going today, almost 400 years later. In the north aisle are a fine eighteenth century oak chest and a rare oil painting dated 1645.

Although still rather gloomy inside it must have been much worse before the south and west galleries were removed. There are two royal coats of arms, the Elizabethan one being unusual in that it is made of hard plaster.

The churchyard was in Malling Street. It was dismantled, and the remains moved to the town's municipal cemetery in the 1970s, to create an approach to Cuilfail Tunnel. In 2000 the floodwater reached a height of six feet and even now sandbags are kept close to the doors at all times. The weathervane on the tower is dated 1756 and inscribed with the initials of the churchwardens of the time. Next to the church is the village pump dated 1804.

LEWES (SOUTH MALLING) *St Michael* OSSA 85 🏛🏛 🍁 ☆☆

There are some very interesting aspects to this church, both historically and in its architecture. The first Malling church stood about half a mile to the north and was one of the oldest in Sussex dating back to the 7th century. There was a Benedictine college at Malling at that time and the first church was part of the monastic group of buildings.

In 1158 a church was built on the present site and at least the lower part of the tower may be from this time. This church was surrendered to Henry VIII in 1545 and pulled down some years later. In 1624 the diarist John Evelyn, then a boy of eight years, laid the foundation stone for the present building. Very few churches were being built at this time and the style reflects the Puritan beliefs of the church's benefactors and the first incumbent. The founders of this church had strong Puritan, American connections and the church resembles many of the early churches in New England.

There is another American connection for John Harvard, founder of Harvard University, was married here in 1636 to the daughter of the vicar of Ringmer church.

Sadly the Victorians replaced the rare plain square windows but the porch is original and carries the church's completion date of 1628. Of the many memorials one stands out as unique, for it recalls the only fatal avalanche recorded in England, which in 1836 killed eight people from Boulder Row in South Street, Lewes, where the event is still remembered in the local pub's name, The Snowdrop.

KINGSTON *St Pancras* OSSA 144 🏛 🍁 ☆

The original grant of land for a church at Kingston is dated 1100, but the church we see today is almost all early thirteenth century. The exception is the tower which is a little out of proportion with the rest of the building and is almost certainly from an earlier building. Following serious lightning damage in the nineteenth century there was extensive restoration with more major work carried out in the 1880s and 1950s.

There is a nice tapsell gate at the boundary wall but the churchyard, although pleasant, has little of interest. The dedication to St Pancras is modern and pays tribute to the original grant of the land from the Priory of St Pancras in Lewes. The original dedication was probably to St Laurence as there is a fifteenth century reference to 'the church of St Laurence in Kingston near Lewes'.

Surviving inside from an earlier church are two small, oddly placed windows and a blocked priest's door. The sockets for the rood beam can be seen set high in the walls.

The splendid chancel arch may also be a leftover from the old building and adds a very airy and spacious feel. The three bells are fifteenth century, two are marked St Mary and St Anne and the third has the bell founder's name, Walter Wimbis. They are hung in a rare, heavily-carved bell frame. Near the font (which may just pre-date the present church) there is an interesting Jacobean carved chest.

IFORD *St Nicholas* OSSA 146 🏛🏛🏛 🍁 ☆

The original church of 1090 consisted of the present nave and a chancel that is now the lower part of the tower. It was built by a Norman knight named Golda. There is not thought to have been a previous Saxon structure on the site, but there is some evidence of an open air field church near by.

The tower, present chancel and north aisle were added in the thirteenth century but the latter was removed within 150 years following the decrease in population brought about by the Black Death. The former north aisle's three blocked pointed arches can be clearly seen both from inside and out. The nave roof is very steep indicating that it was perhaps thatched for much of its life. The present chancel is on a slightly different and more accurate E/W alignment and the upper tower skews round as it rises to match.

The tower contains three of the oldest bells in Sussex dating from about 1426, and the ringers stand at floor level in full view of the congregation. The original west door was blocked in 1886 at the same time as the round-headed west window was changed. At the east end of the nave the Victorians unblocked three very old windows which slightly pre-date the early English lancet style.

The original chancel arch is as good an example of a true Norman arch as you will ever see with its chevron decoration, but the Victorian replacement pillars are best ignored. The long low arch to the north chapel is well worth a look as is the one remaining large stone corbel above the pulpit, which betrays the former position of the rood beam.

RODMELL *St Peter* OSSA 146

hurches are often very close to schools as, originally, many schools were attached to the church. At Rodmell you have to walk through the school playground to get to the church. The church is interesting because at least on the outside it is almost all of the same date, twelfth century. It is not uncommon to find a nave and chancel of this age but at Rodmell the baptistry, south chapel (formally a private chapel for the lord of the manor), the tower and even those usual later additions, the aisles, all date between 1100 and 1200.

The baptistry latched on to the tower is particularly rare and contains its original font, although the four supporting legs are additions. The tower has the steep pyramid cap often seen in the Lewes area, as are the corbelled large pillars with leaf carvings that support the aisles.

Inside the church little remains of great age following the extensive restoration carried out in Victorian times. There is an interesting fifteenth century brass, which has been turned over and used again in the seventeenth century. Almost all the windows are Victorian, the exceptions being the small Norman window (north chancel) and the small windows above the Victorian chancel arch. Above the pulpit is a small window containing some very rare fifteenth century glass depicting the Trinity.

Next to the church is Monks House (owned by The National Trust), the cottage Virginia Woolf and her husband Leonard bought in 1919. She killed herself in 1942 by filling her pockets with large stones, and walking into the nearby Ouse.

SOUTHEASE *St Peter* OSSA 167

outhease has one of the most picturesque churches in all of Sussex. There are records of a church here for more than 1,000 years. The church we see today is eleventh century. It has a round tower built at the same time, or a little before the church — which, by church tower standards, is very old — and is one of only three round towers left in Sussex, all of which are in the Ouse valley.

The river was navigable in Norman times and the tower was almost certainly built for defence against raiders, as it has never had any external access.

The present chancel was once part of the nave of a larger church with aisles, but these, and the original chancel, have long gone. In common with almost all other churches the rood beam was removed after the Reformation, but in the case of Southease it was simply sawn off close to the wall and the projecting stump can still be seen.

There are several Norman windows, including a low one in the tower and a large fourteenth century east window. Once an important church, it had Medieval wall paintings throughout, some of which survive today.

One of the two bells dates from the thirteenth century, and the organ was built *c*1750. The whole building has a simple plain feeling of four stone walls with a wooden roof dropped on top.

PIDDINGHOE *St John* OSSA 168

If asked to select six churches in East Sussex that should be visited I would have to include this one. The church sits on a mound overlooking the river Ouse and has the most impressive of the three round towers in Sussex (all three being within a few miles of each other). It was certainly thriving in 1120 when it was ceded to monks in Lewes, although at that time it consisted of just the nave and tower. The nave was enlarged in the late twelfth century by adding aisles and in the thirteenth century the chancel was built and chancel aisles were added. These were later demolished, with the nave south aisle and it was not until 1882 that the church was restored to its former maximum size.

The interior is particularly dark (but not gloomy) perhaps due to a large number of original windows — old English lancets in deep recesses, a round oculus in the chancel and six small Norman openings in the tower. In contrast to these, but blending in perfectly, is what is considered the best modern window in Sussex. It was designed by M Douglas-Thompson in 1982.

The church is full of interesting, ancient architecture, from the thirteenth century green sandstone font to the Norman round arches of the north aisle. In the churchyard the village stocks can be seen with the original stone supports. This is a reminder that 'God's holy acre' served many uses in ancient times and was a focal point for village life .

On top of the tower's low steep shingle spire is a weathervane in the shape of a trout immortalised in Kipling's 1902 poem *Sussex*.

NEWHAVEN *St Michael* OSSA 179

ewhaven was created from the ancient village of Meeching in the mid- sixteenth century when the Ouse estuary was diverted from Seaford to create a better port. The church, which was built some 300 years earlier, stands high on a hill, with splendid views back along the Ouse towards Lewes, and not suprisingly is dedicated to St Michael as are many churches on hills.

The building consists of a nave of Victorian date interesting only for its very large size, and the original twelfth century tower and apsel chancel which are very interesting indeed. Take off the much later short spire and the east end of the church has hardly changed in 800 years.

Many Norman churches originally had an apse, but these were usually small and formed the far east end of the chancel. Their function as a holy of holies diminished by the end of the Norman period and most were removed, so that now only two or three survive in Sussex. The design of the building seems to have saved the one at Newhaven. Firstly it was large enough to take on the job of chancel, which was useful, because secondly there was no room to build a bigger chancel to the east of the tower as the ground drops away very steeply. So probably by luck and the lie of the land this rare and almost untouched feature has survived. From inside the apse is viewed from the very open and light nineteenth century nave through the somewhat gloomy tower and because of this it has retained its original 'inner sanctum' atmosphere.

TARRING NEVILLE *St Mary* OSSA 168 🏛 🏛 ☆

As the name infers this must have been a Saxon community but the present church is, for the most part, Early English, although with a Transitional Norman south aisle and nave. The exterior church walls are rendered, making this a rare example of what most early churches would have looked like 800 years ago.

All the windows are lancets and match the architecture of the church. Most are original singles or doubles but the triple east window is a modern addition. The tower is the real eye-catcher at this church, being a perfect example of its type — short and sturdy with a low cap.

The nave roof is hung very low with the porch built into it. Inside the church the windows are set in arched recesses and the fourteenth century font is built into the wall, although this was done in the late 1800s. There is an ancient wooden chest in the aisle, said to have come from a wrecked ship of the Spanish Armada.

The churchyard sits on raised ground on the east bank of the river Ouse, in company with a farm but no village. The churchyard is sparsely populated in places adding to the clean lines of the church.

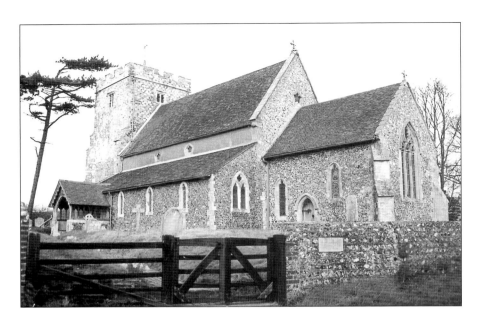

BEDDINGHAM *St Andrew* OSSA 147 🏛 ☆

On the outside only the nave walls remain of the original Norman church, this being a building that has been steadily added to over the years rather than fluctuating in size. This could be because there probably never was a nearby village with changing fortunes to affect the size of the church. The parish was then, as it is now, a spread out farming community.

The sturdy battlemented tower is sixteenth century and is built in an interesting chequered design using stone and flint. The slightly disappointing outside is more then compensated for on the inside where the arcades are the most striking feature. Although these are from the Transitional period (*c*1200) only the south side reflects this as the arches are more pointed on the north side than would be expected. These may have been changed later, however, when the clerestory windows were added during the Decorated period (*c*1290-1350).

The east window also dates from this time while most of the others are earlier lancets: one in the south wall is of that type known as a low side window, the purpose of which has been much debated for many years.

The old font is built into the wall and has hundreds of small crosses carved on it by proud parents over the ages.

DENTON *St Leonard* OSSA 168 ✩

enton certainly had a church in 801AD when a charter confirmed land for it. By the time of the Domesday book, however, Denton showed a village but no church, which may well have been destroyed during the Saxon revolt in 1068, as this area was a strong Saxon centre — the land having been held by King Harold's father Godwin.

Started in the late thirteenth century the present church retains much of its Early English style with some Decorated period parts blending in nicely. The village of Denton, and its church, has been completely surrounded by the modern extension of Newhaven, so much so that it's almost impossible to photograph the church.

In the south wall is a good example of a low side window, often wrongly called a leper window; these windows were almost certainly used to ring a mass bell so people outside the church could know when certain parts of the mass had been reached. There is much evidence for this explanation at Denton. The window is situated in the nave but with a good view of the chancel, and outside the church near the window is a scratch dial for timing the mass.

In the sanctuary is a good example of a tomb used as an Easter sepulchre. The Norman font has a simple weave design very like the one nearby in St Anne's, Lewes. The rector boards on each side of the door are interesting, as they are complete from 1288 to the present day.

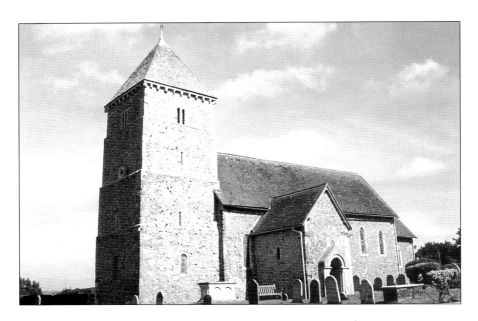

BISHOPSTONE *St Andrew* OSSA 180 🏛🏛🏛 🍁 ☆☆

Bishopstone has avoided the expansion of Seaford and remains a secluded village much as it was 1,200 years ago when the first church was built, although at that time the sea may have reached inland as far as the church.

This may be the oldest church in Sussex, dating back as it does to the eighth century, and much of the existing church is pre-conquest. As the name of the village suggests, this was the seat of a bishop and the large size of the original church reflects this.

The nave and porch (originally a porticus or transept chapel) are pure Saxon; the Norman tower was built early in the twelfth century with interesting string courses separating the four stages and corbels in the shape of grotesque heads. A little later the north aisle and doorway to the porch were added, the doorway being a very fine example of Norman stone carving with a typical Norman zigzag decoration.

The small sanctuary was built in the twelfth century and the last major changes were made in about 1250 when the arcade to the aisle was rebuilt. For the last 700 years the church has remained virtually unchanged. Of particular interest are the Norman font, porch doorway, an early stone coffin lid and a very rare Saxon sundial, showing the sea tides, mounted above the porch door carved with a cross and the name of its probable benefactor, EDRIC.

SEAFORD (EAST BLATCHINGTON) *St Peter* OSSA 180

Despite being part of expanding Seaford, both the village and the church at East Blatchington manage to retain their Downland village atmosphere. The churchyard almost has the look of a garden with its many shrubs, small trees and very well tended grass. There are few gravestones, with a First World War military marker of interest near the east gate. Near the south porch a huge mill stone more than five feet across has been incorporated into the path.

The nave is longer than expected; this is because it is made up of the twelfth century nave and the lower part of the original central tower which was replaced in the thirteenth century by the present west tower. The low tower is topped by a perfect example of a Sussex broach spire. The arches of a former south aisle can be seen on the outside of the present south wall disappearing behind the porch. The nave has a crown post roof containing some ancient tie beams and the Early English chancel has retained its lancet windows.

The priest's doorway has survived with its typical Norman stonework.

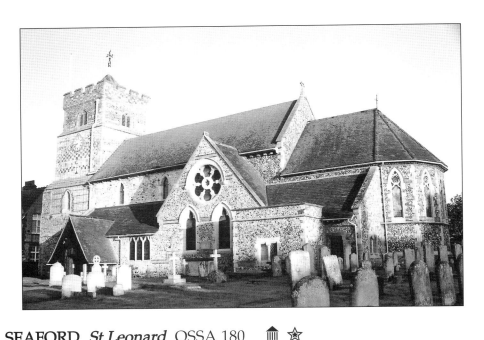

SEAFORD *St Leonard* OSSA 180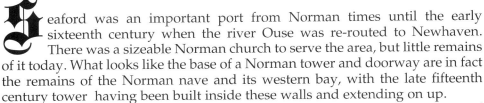

eaford was an important port from Norman times until the early sixteenth century when the river Ouse was re-routed to Newhaven. There was a sizeable Norman church to serve the area, but little remains of it today. What looks like the base of a Norman tower and doorway are in fact the remains of the Norman nave and its western bay, with the late fifteenth century tower having been built inside these walls and extending on up.

Inside the church are some twelfth century pillars, a small ancient carving of St Michael and the dragon and a rare stone coffin and lid. The lids are often seen, and occasionally the coffin, but rarely both together. The lancets in the clerestory were added in the thirteenth century, but the two small windows at the west end are much older.

In the nineteenth century the nave was lengthened and a new chancel, complete with apse, built. Although unusual, and well done, these additions show the Victorians' often complete lack of empathy with an old building. The Perpendicular-style top two stages of the fifteenth century tower are in green sandstone with the stone work being laid with great care to form patterns, the most well defined of which are the three knapped flint crosses just under the clock faces.

The churchyard has relatively few stones for its size but this does not reflect its population. Some churches in Sussex with complete written records record more than 8,000 burials in their churchyards over the centuries.

WEST FIRLE *St Peter* OSSA 148 🏛 🍁 ☆☆

West Firle is approached along a wide, hedge-lined path and is impressive for a medium sized church. The thirteenth century tower, with its huge added buttress, dominates the approach and indeed the whole church. The building has benefited from its close proximity to the medieval manor of Firle Place and many of that house's masters added to the church, leaving us with a building consisting of several medieval styles.

The chancel is contemporary with the tower but the north door is *c*1200 and has been reset in its present location from an earlier church. The clerestory was added in the fourteenth century and the aisles rebuilt in the fifteenth.

The churchyard is tree-lined, heavily populated on the north side, and contains the graves of painters Duncan Grant and Vanessa Bell, artists of the murals in Berwick church. Vanessa Bell was Virginia Woolf's sister.

Inside there are a number of interesting memorials. The church contains some of Sussex's best brasses including a fourteenth century knight in armour and his wife, and the sixteenth century chapel contains three tomb chests, one of which has alabaster figures of Sir John Gage (builder of Firle Place) and his wife.

The church's stained glass is of interest, spanning as it does 400 years. In the south aisle is a fragment of medieval glass depicting the crucifixion, while in the north-east chapel is a twentieth century window showing the tree of life.

The Boundary Wall

On arrival at a church the visitor's first contact is the entrance to the church grounds. All too often this is bypassed quickly in an attempt to reach the main building. This is a great mistake. There is much of interest at the boundary wall. Until the tenth century churchyards were not enclosed, but by the time the Normans arrived in 1066 a boundary wall or fence was becoming the norm and by the seventeenth century it would seem that all churchyards were enclosed.

The upkeep of the boundary was often divided among the congregation according to their standing in the village; those with more land had larger stretches of the fence to maintain than those with less. The churchwarden kept the records. At Chiddingly the records of 1722 show that fifty-six people were charged with the upkeep of the fence, the lengths allocated varying between 3 ft and 43ft.

Many churches have beautiful lych gates. The name means 'corpse gate'. The lych symbolised the gate between life and death, and was where the coffin rested at the beginning of the burial service. None surviving today seem older than seventeenth century and one of the earliest in the country is at Hartfield, where the gate is built into an old half-timbered cottage.

These are the most striking churchyard entrances but many other interesting portals are to be found. At Pevensey a slot stile just wide enough to walk through is to be seen in the boundary wall nearer to the castle than the main

The lych gate at Hartfield

The tapsell gate at Friston

church gate. An obvious short cut big enough for people, but not wide enough to allow animals to get in or, for that matter, out, as many Sussex churches still to this day graze sheep in their churchyards to keep the grass down. Chailey has another type of style, this one going over the wall and with a nice round footplate on the low side. At Friston the main gate is a central pivoting tapsell gate, a type unique to Sussex, and which also seems to have more to do with moving animals in and out than people.

A particularly nice idea is the pair of iron memorial gates at Chalvington. The gates are the village's memorial to those who fell in the Second World War, and they do their job admirably, as it is hard to enter the churchyard without thinking of those men.

Look too for private gates, which led to castles, parsonages, manor houses.

The lych gate at Waldron

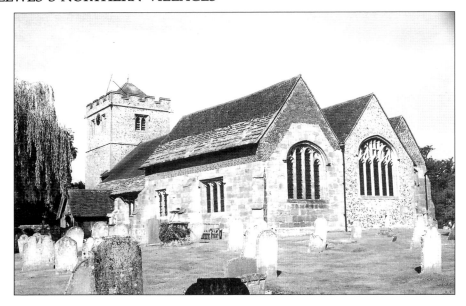

RINGMER *St Mary the Virgin* OSSA 124 ☆

The only clues to the original church at Ringmer are the pillar bases, which are possibly twelfth century, and thirteenth century nave arches. Sir Herbert Whalley gave the fine painted metal prayer boards at the east end of the nave in 1684. At the west end is an organ gallery built in the 1930s but containing much older carvings which came from nearby Glyndebourne. The south chapel is early sixteenth century and retains its piscina, although the altar it served has long gone. On the wall here is a bassoon, the last vestige of the orchestra that provided music from an earlier west gallery prior to the coming of the organ in 1856. Dole boards record charities which, after almost 400 years, are still active.

In the nave are a memorial to members of the village cricket team who died on active service, and a monument to Peter Meshullam, British consul in Jerusalem, who was murdered near Bethlehem in the nineteenth century. There are some good seventeenth century memorials, two with American connections — to Harbert Springett whose daughter married William Penn, founder of Pennsylvania, and to John Sadler, vicar of Ringmer, whose daughter Anne married John Harvard, founder of Harvard University. The massive door (ask to see the huge key) leads to a fifteenth century porch with some original timbers. There are two rare wooden graveboards, recently restored, and at the far east end of the churchyard is a marker to Mary Stonehouse, known as 'the butcher's stone', because the indent on the side was caused by a village butcher in the 1800s sharpening his knives.

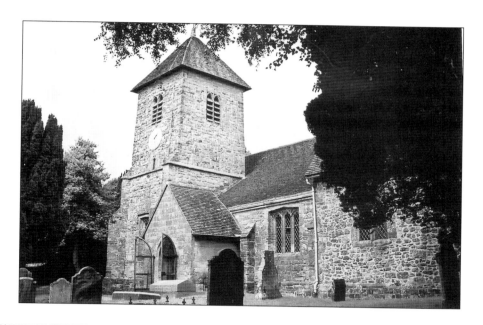

WIVELSFIELD *St Peter and St John the Baptist* OSSA 74

Wivelsfield's church is of a sandy ironstone construction and dates from the eleventh century. An ancient doorway from this period, with a fine rounded arch top remains, but was moved to its present position in the north wall in the 1800s. Three windows now in the north aisle were moved from their more important position as the main east windows at the same time.

The two-stage tower is probably the same height today as when it was built in 1500, and has a nice pyramid cap. The porch seems to be a later addition and does little to enhance the look of the church.

The churchyard is wooded around the church, but opens up into a large area to the west. Members of the famous Sussex family of iron founders, the Fullers (see Brightling), can be found to the south-west, with iron graveboards in near mint condition. There is one military marker dated 1946, but perhaps the most interesting stone is near the church door and marks the grave of a man who served his country in the CIV (City of London Imperial Volunteers) during the South African war, on a cycle. The machines used were twelve-seaters, adapted to run on railway tracks.

Inside the church there is a good trefoil-headed piscina and in the north wall a rare aumbry. The pulpit has carving from the Jacobean period but the pulpit itself is older.

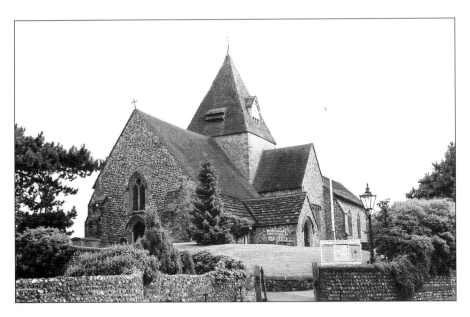

DITCHLING *St Margaret* OSSA 98   🏛 🏛 🍁 ☆

This large cruciform church of very pleasing proportions stands on a high mound in the middle of the village in the shadow of Ditching Beacon. The village has been an important one for hundreds of years and the growth of the church and the use of some Caen stone (brought from Normandy) in its building reflect this.

The nave is the oldest part, being eleventh century, the rest is thirteenth with the exception of the north transept, which is Victorian and was probably built specifically to house the organ.

The east window is very good with its label stops in the shape of royal heads and slim stone shafts with carved capitals. These shafts are repeated in the lancets of the north wall. The different building periods come together at the crossing where at least three styles are evident especially in the pillars. The south chapel has a memorial dated 1580 and a very intricate window.

The churchyard is not overcrowded and drops away sharply to the west where ruins of an ancient building can be seen. It is hard to find a bad spot to photograph this church although a modern glass porch on the north side should be avoided at all costs

The parish chest at Arlington

Food jar and stone coffin slab, Arlington

The rood screen at Berwick

The north aisle at Berwick

Tomb of Richard Leche, High Sheriff of Sussex and Surrey, and his wife, at Fletching

The font at Arlington

Inscribed gutter at Brede

The Jefferay memorial, Chiddingly

WESTMESTON *St Martin* OSSA 120 ☆

The nave at Westmeston is Norman and retains its Norman north doorway. The attached porch contains some very old timbers (fourteenth century) but the brick base is much later. In the churchyard is a very fine example of a large Victorian tomb in excellent condition.

However, inside the church the Victorians have much to answer for as only small copies of what must have been incredible medieval wall paintings remain following rebuilding work carried out in the 1860s. The stained glass dates from this time and was made by Clayton and Bell who made windows for many Sussex churches; it is not their best work but is still good.

On the wall by the door is a rare lead memorial inlaid with an enamel coat of arms for a Rifle Brigade officer killed in action in 1915. The fourteenth century south arcade is so large it appears more like another nave than an arcade with the high arcade arches adding to this impression. The Norman font is an unusual cup shape and not as heavy as most fonts of its period.

PLUMPTON *St Michael and All Angels* OSSA 121 🏛🏛 ☆☆

Plumpton church could easily be missed, sitting as it does so far back from the road, and this would be a shame as it is a gem. On the site of a pre-conquest church, the present one dates from as early as the eleventh century. The nave and south door are the oldest parts, with the tower and chancel added in the thirteenth century. The buttress and west door came a little later and, as seems common in this area, the brick porch is sixteenth century. The east chancel wall was rebuilt when the vestry was added in Victorian times.

The churchyard boasts two ancient yews and is sparsely populated with gravemarkers.

Inside the church the medieval wall paintings, uncovered in 1955, are particularly interesting (those that survived the Victorians). Note the scroll decorations around the surviving Norman window which give a good idea how bright the inside of a medieval church would have been.

The prayer and commandment boards on the west wall date from the late 1700s. An unusual feature of the church is the roof lining, which is made up of pieces of old pews.

EAST CHILTINGTON OSSA 99 🏛 🍁 ☆

ast Chiltington may have started life as a church, but at some time before 1291 it became a chapel of ease and stayed that way for 600 years, becoming a parish church in 1909 when, for the first time, it gained a churchyard.

The church carries no dedication, although it almost certainly did prior to becoming a chapel. Of the twelfth century Norman church there remains the south door, a now blocked north door, one window and much of the nave walls. The thirteenth century tower has walls three feet thick and seems to have retained its original height, which is exactly the same as the nave ridge; the added Sussex cap suits it well.

The chancel is fourteenth century and contains some interesting modern items, including a bishop's chair dated 1929. Of great interest in the nave are several charity boards, the oldest dated 1611. The pulpit is dated 1719. Pulpits from the eighteenth century are very rare, there being probably only two or three in the county.

The single bell is dated 1769 and hangs in an ancient frame which shows evidence of a thirteenth century predecessor. The lych gate was added soon after the churchyard in 1913 (look to the underside of the lych gate roof for interesting evidence of recent benefactors to its restoration). The yew tree has witnessed the whole history of the church, having been scientifically dated at 1,200 years old and it may be the reason the church was built on the knoll in the first place.

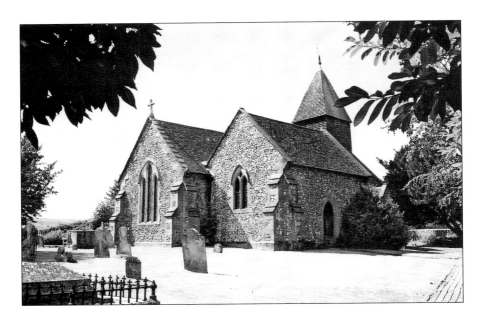

STREAT OSSA 99

The Romans built their roads straight, and for hundreds of years after they left these were the only reasonable roads in England, and were called straights. In the course of time the word changed to the modern word for a road, street. So it is no surprise to find that the village of Streat sits square on a Roman road.

The Norman church was built on the site of one of two Saxon churches in the area, but little of the Norman building remains, let alone the Saxon, following heavy restoration in the late nineteenth century when the Norman doorways were lost.

The church is quite small and pleasing to the eye, but has no outstanding features on the outside or in the churchyard. Inside there are two interesting iron graveslabs set into the floor. One is thought to be the largest in the country. It is well written and has three dates marked from the mid-eighteenth century. The other was cast by a different craftsman — the words change size as they progress, run into each other without a space and end with the '3' in the date written backwards. A reminder perhaps that although skilled craftsmen, most journeymen could not read or write and worked from a list they simply copied without understanding a word.

There are some good wall tablets also from the eighteenth century and the royal arms of Charles II dated 1660 above the chancel arch.

HAMSEY *St Peter* OSSA 12 🏛 🍁 🍁 ☆

he church at Hamsey now stands alone, with even the river Ouse having returned to its original course leaving the nearby bridge high and dry most of the year. With the village moving to favour the road rather than the river, a new church at Offham was built in Victorian times. Unusually for the Victorians, and luckily for us, the old church was neither demolished nor de-consecrated and is still in use on rare occasions.

The churchyard contains some interesting old gravestones, including one with a 1722 date showing crossbones with a pick and shovel design. The church is early twelfth century retaining its Norman nave and chancel but with a much later fourteenth century tower in the Perpendicular style.

Under the battlemented top there are large gargoyles of note. The tower is spoiled by the blocking up of most of the upper openings, some in centuries past, but presumably most were closed when the bells were moved to the new church. The lower third of the roof still consists of Horsham stone slabs.

The porch is a good sixteenth century example and leads to an interesting interior free from Victorian restoration. The chancel arch is a simple Norman one, but rare to have survived unaltered. The chancel was extended in about 1350 and the east window dates from this time.

There is a large tomb chest dated 1538 and some good funeral hatchments on the walls together with the arms of George III. The font is of limestone and is probably fifteenth century

BARCOMBE *St Mary the Virgin* OSSA 101 ☆

Barcombe church is in about as picturesque a setting as it is possible to be. It sits high on the Ouse valley with excellent views towards Lewes with just a well-kept farm, a couple of houses and a large pond for company (the village having been re-sited a mile or so away after a visitation of the Black Death in the seventeenth century).

The churchyard is extensive with some interesting old stones — more than thirty of which have been built into the south wall of the church. The oldest remaining part of the building is the north wall (eleventh century). The very short tower is thirteenth century and inside there is evidence of the church being enlarged, as the south arcade is older at the east end (being thirteenth century) whereas the west end is about 100 years later.

There is a huge 1730 marble memorial with life-sized figures dominating the south wall, and set into the tower arch is a nicely done, recent engraved glass screen. Much of the stained glass came from the well-known Victorian workshop of Clayton and Bell, who were responsible for many Sussex windows including Ardingly and Westmeston.

The old chestnut pulpit was given to the church in 1790, but removed during the Victorian restoration in 1879 and given to Willingdon Museum; recently it was returned to the church. There are two ancient chests, one a typical parish chest with three locks, the other is Spanish and has a complex twelve ward lock, all worked by one key. One or two of these Spanish chests exist in the south of England and are often said to be salvage from the Armada.

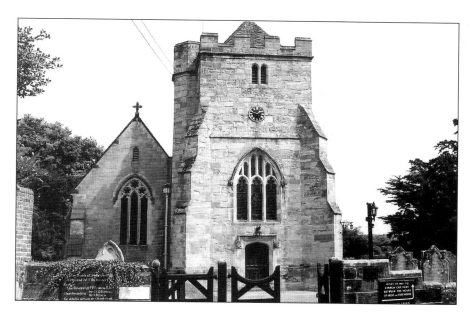

NEWICK *St Mary* OSSA 76 🏛 ⭐⭐

The first known priest of Newick was Richard Le Waithe in 1288, but there was a church here long before that. The oldest remaining area to be seen today is the south wall on either side of the porch. This dates from about 1080, as does the small Norman window to the right of the porch. This window was bricked up at some stage but was reopened and glazed in the nineteenth century.

The porch is early fourteenth century and amazingly contains much of its original timber. It was almost certainly moved from the west end of the church when the tower was built in the fifteenth century. The thirteenth century chancel completes the 400 years of additions.

The church has a rare Jacobean pulpit, with an original lantern bracket nearby, and some fourteenth century glass in the medallions in the two south wall windows. Like the porch the roof contains some medieval timbers. The organ is particularly worthy of note being perhaps the only complete Casson organ in existence. These were built by Thomas Casson, a retired banker, especially for country churches where the organists were of limited skill. The keyboard contains the pedalboard actions, making it easier to play. These organs were years ahead of their time in design.

The six bells replaced much older bells in 1867 and carry the inscription 'Rejoice with them that do rejoice and weep with them that weep'.

The churchyard has some old stones, many placed against the east boundary wall when the chancel was extended in the nineteenth century.

CHAILEY *St Peter* OSSA 75 ☆

The boundary wall at Chailey has one of those interesting additional entrances you often find, usually designed to allow access while either keeping the lawn-mowing sheep in, or unwanted farm animals out. This one takes the form of a stone style with a very interesting round stone foot support on the lower side. This is quite close to the main gate, which might suggest that the present main gate is in a relatively new spot.

The church is built of a light ironstone often seen in parts of Sussex, which always gives a bright, crisp, newly cut look. The tower dominates the church, or perhaps it would be more correct to say the spire dominates, for it is as tall as the tower, if not taller. The spire is steep-sided with belfry openings, one carrying a nice clock.

The chancel, north arcade and tower are thirteenth century — the latter being interesting because, whereas most towers have had parts added to make them taller, this one seems to be of its original height with just the spire added. The unusual angle buttresses are clearly of a later date.

Inside, Victorian restoration prevails and the royal coat of arms in the north aisle is that of Queen Victoria, although more modern than many you see; these particular arms are quite rare in Sussex churches. There is an interesting eighteenth century iron grave slab now set in the tower, and in the churchyard more seventeenth century stones than usual seem to have survived, perhaps because of their unusual great weight and thickness.

CHURCHYARDS

The perfect example of peace and tranquillity must surely be the churchyard of an English village church in high summer. This quiet place is also a history book overflowing with clues to the past of the church, village and surrounding area, and should be explored with great care.

First and foremost this was the piece of land chosen to build an early Christian church, in some cases well over 1,000 years ago. If the church was to succeed the builders had to get it right, and the clues to their success can often be found in the churchyard. When Christianity was first beginning to establish itself in England, with the backing of the church in Rome, Pope Gregory I sent a letter with Bishop Augustine to England telling him to destroy all places of pagan worship. However, before he even arrived in England the order was rescinded and replaced with another ordering Augustine to use areas sacred to non-Christian religions in the spreading of Christianity.

In this second letter the Pope observed that people would 'continue to frequent the same sacred places' even if dedicated to a new God. Churches were often built on ground where non-Christians already worshipped and the evidence is often still there to be seen. Many churchyards contain ancient yew trees (or the stumps of those that did not survive the hurricane of 1987). The yew was often the focal point of pre-Christian worship; considered the tree of life, it is the origin of the yule log and, it is said, of the Christmas tree. The yew in St Mary's churchyard at Wilmington has been scientifically dated as being

The churchyard at Arlington

The 1,600-year-old yew at Wilmington

more than 1,600 years old, and the site may have been a place of worship long before the church took over. The tree is now held together with chains and props but is very much alive and stands almost in conflict with the church, as if trying to outlast the competition.

At Selmeston the churchyard is round, which is unusual (there are perhaps four in Sussex) and may indicate a pre-Christian Saxon burial ground. Several churches, such as Alciston and Friston, are built on ancient burial mounds, which were clearly sacred areas long before the Christian church arrived.

Headstones did not appear until the seventeenth century. This was because a churchyard was not, then, solely a burial area, but also a place for church festivals, village fairs, markets, meetings or even army musters and practices. At Berwick worn patches on the church wall show where arrows were sharpened. Many sports took place in the churchyard and were actually encouraged as legitimate pastimes after divine service by James I in his *Book of Sports* written in 1617. Some churchyards still contain a cockfighting pit, although there are none in East Sussex.

Before headstones became common, grave markers were few and reserved for prominent people, usually inside the church. The village people were simply buried in the churchyard with no marker, or perhaps a wooden one that soon rotted away, but more likely one large marker to stand for everyone. It is worth noting that from earliest times graveyards were re-used time and time again. Some churches with complete records can list more than 8,000 burials over the centuries. The earliest markers took the form of a flat or slightly raised slab forming the top of a stone coffin in a shallow grave.

Sometimes they were outside the church but more often set in the earth floor inside with the lid protruding. Many may still be found today, often set against the walls of the church or, as in the case of the rare iron slab at Rotherfield, inside the church.

The oldest headstones are usually to be found close to the church on the east or south side. The north side, if used at all, often contains the latest graves, as for many years the north was considered the dark and least holy direction and was in some cases used only for criminals, suicides and murderers. A good example is at Patcham where a grave on the north side is for a smuggler and reads 'unfortunately shot'.

Most grave markers remaining today are of stone, but Sussex still has a number of the earlier wooden graveboards, notably at Westfield and Chiddingly. There are also many iron markers — a link to the county's long history as the centre of the iron industry.

There are interesting stone markers at Friston and Maresfield, in the shape of wooden grave boards, a transitional design perhaps. Most gravestones in churchyards face east, this is probably intentional as it makes them easier to read as the rotating sun casts a better shadow into the stonemasons' incised letters.

Even flora and fauna in a churchyard are worthy of note; in many cases a churchyard has been protected from the outside world for hundreds of years and certain wild flowers are virtually extinct outside of them. This in turn encourages insects, butterflies, birds and small animals to enjoy the peace and protection of the boundary wall. It is even thought that some species of butterfly exist only in a few churchyards where the particular wild flowers they need still grow.

Prior to the Reformation many churchyards also had gardens attached, for the growing of flowers for the church as well as vegetables for the priest. These gardens disappeared at the same time as the brightly painted church interiors and elaborate ceremonies, as part of the more puritan Protestant view of Christianity.

With trees it is a different story. Other than the ancient oaks and yews that often pre-date the church, and churches built in woodland such as at Houghton, churchyards rarely had trees in them. Early drawings and plans show no trees in churchyards that now abound in them. The planting of trees seems to have coincided with the fashion for landscape gardens in the mid-eighteenth century. The long straight rows of trees at Whatlington are clearly planned and planted by man rather than nature.

So take your time crossing the churchyard, sometimes it can be at least as interesting as the church in the middle.

ALCISTON OSSA 170 ☆☆

Alciston church now stands in some seclusion, but in the twelfth century this was an important monastic settlement. Close to the church the remains of a grange belonging to Battle Abbey can still be seen incorporated into a farmhouse, as well as a tithe barn and fourteenth century dovecote. A Norman window remains on the north side of the chancel and remains of a pre-conquest apse were found near the west window during restoration work. The apse must have been destroyed when the chancel was built. The chancel was changed in the twelfth century and shortened in the fifteenth and the remains of a third Early English lancet window at the west end of the north wall shows that the chancel must have extended some way before that time. Outside the blocked priest's door no less than five scratch dials can be seen on the jambs. These crudely-cut sundials allowed the priests to time the various parts of the mass. Another dial can be found on a stone east of the porch.

Also on this stone are the marks of arrows being sharpened. This, also seen at Berwick church, is a reminder that churchyards had many uses in medieval times, including the mustering and training of archers. It is recorded that archers from this area fought at Agincourt.

The porch door is mostly fifteenth century and was lucky to avoid the rather drastic Victorian restoration of the church interior in 1853. Just inside the sanctuary rail two seventeenth century ledger slabs have survived, as have the two late fourteenth century bells that hang in the turret at the west end of the nave. The two oak beams reaching up from the floor support this bell turret.

ALFRISTON *St Andrew* OSSA 170 🏛🏛 🍁🍁 ☆☆

This cruciform church, built in the shape of a Greek cross, is often referred to as 'the Cathedral of the Downs' because of its sheer size — 115ft long and 70ft wide at the crossing. It is unusual in that it is almost all original fourteenth century, with no additions. There must have been an earlier church, for this was a large Saxon settlement, but nothing remains.

The present building is mostly flint which is so finely cut and positioned that the work is considered some of the best in England. There is a spectacular sedilia to one side of the chancel and an Easter sepulchre on the other. There are unusual carved heads above the sepulchre. The windows are especially interesting as they were built at a time of architectural change and reflect the transition from the Decorated (chancel) to Perpendicular styles. Almost all the glass is modern with just a little old glass in the upper part of the north transept depicting St Alphege.

There are no aisles, which means a wide crossing with high heavy arches needed to support the central tower. The pillars of the arches have an interesting fluted design which was hidden under plaster until the mid-nineteenth century. Unique surviving features are the Lenten veil hooks on the eastern-most beam in the chancel. These were used to hang the Lenten veil to hide the altar during Lent in pre-Reformation times. The royal coat of arms is that of George I, and the nearby hatchment is for the Vincent family. Few memorials can be found inside the church and this is thought to be because there was never a lord of the manor or major family attached to Alfriston.

BERWICK *St Michael and All Angels* OSSA 170 🏛 🍁🍁 ☆☆☆

Berwick church is built on a pre-Christian burial mound, artefacts from which can be found in the Barbican Museum at Lewes, and although the present building is twelfth century it stands on the site of previous structures, the early ones probably of wood. A number of churches running east-west were built on these mounds, another indication of the original builders using existing sacred ground as sites for their churches.

The oldest feature is the font, which is certainly from an earlier church and could be close to 1,000 years old. Near the font marks can be seen on the tower where archers sharpened their arrows prior to practising at the nearby butts. The churchyard has some old stones and there is a mounting block in the car park.

What Berwick is famous for, however, is its wall paintings. Following the loss of most of the stained glass due to bomb blast in 1940, it was decided to put in clear glass and cover the walls with murals and plasterboard paintings in the old style. Bloomsbury artists Vanessa Bell, Duncan Grant and Quentin Bell, who lived nearby at Firle, were commissioned to do the work. An excellent guidebook to the paintings is available in the church.

In the early nineteenth century this church was described as almost derelict. The north aisle was bricked up because the roof had collapsed, the tower was in ruins, with the bells broken on the floor and earth piled as high as the windows of the nave — but now it is in good order and offers a unique view of an almost lost art.

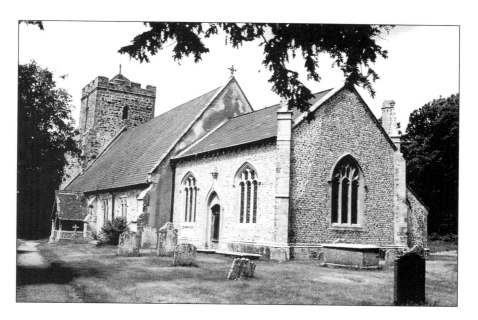

LAUGHTON *All Saints* OSSA 126 🏛 ☆☆

aughton was the seat of that famous family of Sussex church tower benefactors, the Pelhams, and has one of the best examples of that particular way of being remembered. As usual the Pelham buckle can be found on the tower, this time as the label stops on the west door. The buckle represents the sword buckle of the King of France who was captured by Sir John Pelham at Poitiers in 1356. The family vault is situated under the chancel and contains thirty-five coffins whose occupants include one bishop, two Prime Ministers, three earls and a duke. It was finally sealed in 1886.

The nave is the oldest part of the building and retains two original lancets; the other windows are in the Perpendicular style. The eighteenth century chancel is at a slightly different angle to the nave. Although this quite common occurrence is said to represent the angle of Christ's head on the cross, it probably indicates a more accurate east-west alignment of the later chancel as a result of more modern measuring equipment. This is a rare example of early Gothic Revival; also noteworthy is the priest's doorway with its ogee arch.

The war memorial for the 1914-18 war dominates the inside, which has few old memorials. There is a small plaque to parishioners killed by a flying bomb in the Second World War, a reminder of the large number of these first guided missiles that were brought down in Sussex.

Traces of the rood screen can be seen under the chancel arch and part of the screen has been re-used behind the altar. High up hang two funeral helms and the royal arms of George III.

51

RIPE *St John the Baptist* OSSA 126 🏛🏛 ✰✰

The imposing church at Ripe is basically of three periods, the oldest parts (the porch and nave) date from the thirteenth century with the chancel being mid-fourteenth and the Pelham tower fifteenth century. The carvings on and around the porch are of great interest as is the large fourteenth century holy water stoup. On the buttress east of the porch is a scratch dial, a roughly carved sundial used in medieval times to gauge the correct timing of the mass.

The nave is large, high and well proportioned, though a little austere. The rood screen and loft are long gone but the entrance and high exit to the blocked rood stairs are clearly visible to the east. The font (much restored) is from about 1400. Of particular interest is the large east window of plain glass but with ten separate inserts of fourteenth century glass and one small piece with a Tudor rose motif. The window itself has very fine tracery.

The churchyard is well populated, with some interesting stones, but it is the massive battlemented tower that dominates the exterior. There are many of these towers in this part of Sussex, built by the Pelham family all within 100 years of each other, and all very much the same. Usually the Pelham buckle can be found in part of the stonework; at Ripe it is the label stops on the west door.

SELMESTON *St Mary* OSSA 149 🍁 ☆

elmeston church is believed to be dedicated to St Mary and had extensive rebuilding in 1867. Paintings inside the church show the building as it was and it is clear that the present building follows the lines of the old with even the windows being copies of the originals. Little remains of earlier structures and there have certainly been many.

The churchyard is unusual in being round, and this is often an indication of Saxon or even pre-Christian use.

The building is a simple two-cell type with a shingled bell turret at the west end and the typical Sussex low sloping roof on the south side. The nineteenth century entrance, in common with many Sussex churches where changes have been made, is set in the north wall and one of the few remaining medieval details, the west door, is blocked off. A holy water stoup, a thirteenth century piscina and an Easter sepulchre survive along with an interesting brass in the south aisle to Henry Rogers (1639) inscribed 'a painefull Preacher in this church two & thirty yeeres'.

The fourteenth century wooden arcade between the nave and the south aisle is very rare and the nineteenth century font appears to be a copy of a broken thirteenth century one found under the lych gate when it was rebuilt.

ARLINGTON *St Pancras* OSSA 150

There has been a village very near the church since Roman times and a church on this site for more than 1,000 years. Although the present nave is itself largely Saxon, evidence of an earlier wooden structure and an even earlier wattle and daub building, both destroyed by fire, were found during restoration work.

In the churchyard there are some interesting old stones with odd carvings close to the south wall of the chancel. Very close to the porch one Saxon window with Roman tiles for its arch survives of the original six.

Of the early Norman additions the chapel, with its superb dog tooth corbel forming the arch spring, has many interesting items including an ancient food jar found under the floor, and some very old graveslabs originally in the floor and now fixed to the walls. To the north west is a fine medieval church chest. During the transitional period the tower and the low side window were added. About 1250 the Saxon north wall was lost when the aisle was added to accommodate the increased population and the chancel was largely rebuilt.

By 1850 the church was described as 'in total ruin' and when the Reverend Thomas Bunston became vicar it was hardly usable. He set about raising the money and restoring the church in a way that preserved its ancient features, a rare idea in those days. So we must thank him for saving the fifteenth century roof, which is second to none, the sixteenth century murals (fragments only) and the seventeenth century bells, which were restored and re-hung for the 1893 re-opening. Bunston's memorial is in the chancel.

CHALVINGTON *St Bartholomew* OSSA 150 🏛🏛 ☆

There is no record of a church at Chalvington in the Domesday book (1086) but it was one of the churches taxed by the Pope in 1291, and it is thought that it was built a little before that date and that there was no earlier structure on the site. The church is small and simple and with very few changes from the original style.

The east window was added about 1400 and the bell turret some time after that. The roof and door are said to be thirteenth century and the latter was moved to its present position (where it is protected by a modern porch) from the north side where the blocked doorway is clearly visible.

The building is of flint with stone quoins and rendered with plaster. It should be noted that most village churches were rendered with plaster in medieval times and Chalvington offers a chance to see how it would have appeared then.

There is quite a lot of old stained glass, one of the two high triangular lights to the east has a fragment and the east window contains an inscription stating that it was the gift of a rector's widow in 1409. The oldest glass is in the north-east nave window and is believed to be of Thomas a Becket; it could be the oldest in Sussex, being thirteenth century. There is some evidence that the original church dedication was to Becket. The font is fifteenth century and the piscina thirteenth century. The three bells are all early seventeenth century.

The churchyard has few interesting stones but the iron gates at the front are the church's war memorial for local men, while the back gates remember the son of the benefactors (the Bayleys), a sailor lost on HMS *Martin* in 1942.

EAST DEAN *St Simon and St Jude* OSSA 183

Very picturesquely situated in a deep hollow, St Simon and St Jude has all the hallmarks of a church that has grown along with the village over a very long period. The oldest part is the tower, at least part of which is Saxon. In common with many early churches near the sea or large rivers, it was almost certainly used as a defensive refuge against raiders, and the walls are three feet thick. It formed the nave of an early church and led to an apse in the east wall. The blocked arch leading to the apse can still be seen.

The remains of other Norman arches, and a now-covered pillar shaft may indicate that the church was cruciform in shape when the present nave was built in the twelfth century. The chancel was added a little later, possibly early thirteenth century, and is a little out of line with the nave — being inclined more correctly to the east. This is not uncommon with chancels added at this time and probably represents a better ability to orientate the building correctly rather than the common explanation that it represents the angle of Christ's head on the cross. The baptistry is modern, as is the font, although the latter is modelled on an earlier Norman one, of which a fragment has been included.

An ornate Jacobean pulpit with sounding board is dated 1623 and this and the massive fifteenth century tie beam roof dominate the interior. There is also a fine holy water stoup.

The churchyard has a typical Sussex tapsell gate and in the north-east corner, a sad reminder of the Second World War, are the graves of two unknown seamen washed up on the coast and inscribed simply 'Known unto God'.

FRISTON *St Mary the Virgin* OSSA 134 🏛 🍁 ☆☆

A blocked doorway and window in the south wall are all that remain of the pre-conquest Saxon church that stood on this ancient piece of land on Downland a mile inland from the Seven Sisters.

Despite regular additions, starting in the twelfth century when the nave was enlarged, the building retains its basic two-cell format with a few extras such as the tiled bell turret at the west end. Two Norman doorways remain in the porch and vestry, and in the fourteenth century chancel there are an aumbry, a piscina and a reredos recess — but the star of the interior is the fifteenth century tie-beam roof with large crown posts.

Memorials to the Selwyn family are much in evidence, a large one to Thomas (died 1613) shows him in alabaster with several new-born babies and six daughters below, the former being an indication of the high infant mortality rate of those times.

The churchyard is well kept and entered by one of the best examples of that unique Sussex portal, a tapsell gate. Here, there is a reminder of the proximity of the sea, a simple wooden cross marked only 'Washed ashore'.

LITLINGTON *St Michael the Archangel* OSSA 182

This small church is a good example of a Norman village church, for most of the nave and chancel are original twelfth century. Only the western end of the nave, with its weatherboarded bell tower, porch (both fourteenth century) and the vestry (nineteenth century) are later additions. On the north side of the tower an angled jutting wall has two mass dials facing in different directions, both are divided into twenty-four divisions. It was originally thought that they had been moved to this position, but it has since been established that the sun does give accurate readings on the two faces at different times of the year. There is another dial on the south porch.

Two windows in the north wall are Norman, as are the south doorway and the string course on both the north and south nave walls. The beams supporting the roof are thought to be of very great age, possibly even thirteenth century, and are roughly hewn.

Inside it is clear that the floor level has changed for there is a slope of 13in from east to west, and the thirteenth century piscina and sedilia in the chancel are unusually high. Once again the Victorians have much to answer for. During their 1863 'restoration' the ancient oak screen and stone tympanum in the chancel arch, and the three lancet windows in the east wall were lost. Most of the glass is modern but that in the Norman north nave windows may be thirteenth century, and depict the four Evangelists. One of the three bells (the treble) is very old; it was cast at the Whitechapel foundry by William Chamberlain about 1450 and carries a Latin inscription in black letters.

LULLINGTON OSSA 171

This church is often called the smallest in Sussex, or one of the smallest in England, and while true the descriptions are a little misleading. For although it is only about five metres square, and is a fully functioning church complete with bell, this is in fact the chancel of a much larger church whose foundations can still be seen west of the present entrance.

It is not known for sure when the church was destroyed, but local legend says it was in Cromwell's time. The church dates from the thirteenth century and is in the Early English style; the window in the north wall is of that date, the others being fourteenth century.

The church stands on a hill overlooking the Cuckmere river and can be reached only by steep footpaths. The dedication was lost when the church was destroyed, but a sixteenth century Will lists among the bequests 'a taper set before St Sithe in the church of the same'.

The building was repaired and made suitable for services in 1806, and the bell turret must have been added at that time for the bell carries the same date. The church can seat twenty, although double that has been squeezed in at harvest festival. It is believed that in the mid-1930s a copy of the church was built, by a Sussex architect, as a war memorial in the USA, but his patrons would not allow him to say where.

JEVINGTON *St Andrew* OSSA 183 🏛🏛 ☆

evington was a village in Saxon times and the church reflects this. Much of the large squat tower is of that era, dating from about 900. Two Saxon windows (now blocked) can still be identified by their recycled Roman tile arches, and the lower part of the tower contains some good long and short work. View the tower from the inside to get a real feel of its age. The original baluster shafts were re-used in the belfry openings during restoration work carried out on the tower in the nineteenth century; the lancet tower windows date from this restoration.

A north aisle was added to the nave in the thirteenth century, piercing the much older north wall; it contains good examples of lancet windows of the Early English period. In the north wall is a rare Saxon church carving, found during restoration work on the tower, depicting a holy figure thrusting a staff into the mouth of a monster. Similar carvings occur elsewhere in Sussex and are probably of St Michael and the dragon. During this same restoration the squints were straightened and look a little out of place.

The chancel has a trefoil topped piscina of the rarer shelved type and there is an aumbry in the north wall. In the chancel is an interesting memorial to a former rector, Nathaniel Collier, with the date given as 1691/2; the date on which the New Year began was in dispute at that time, because of the changeover from the Julian to the Gregorian calendar, and the date reflects this. The Tudor wagon roof in the nave is part hammer beam, part crown post. One of the bells is interesting, as it is clearly a ship's bell.

WEST DEAN *All Saints* OSSA 182   🏛🏛 🍁 ☆☆

The most striking feature of the church is the short rectangular tower with its gabled cap, often referred to as a 'monks hood', which is unique in Sussex. The side buttresses add to the wide appearance of the tower and give the whole church a very pleasing aspect.

The nave and lower tower are twelfth century and much of the rest fourteenth, including the chancel which is the same width as the nave. The clear division between the two was the rood screen, which was not removed until the 1840s.

Almost in ruins in the seventeenth century, the building is now in near perfect condition and contains some interesting memorials. Two busts are the most unusual —one by Clair Sheridan of Sir Oswald Birley, the painter, unveiled by Lady Churchill in 1958, and the other by Epstein of John Anderson, Viscount Waverley, unveiled by Prime Minister Harold Macmillan in 1960. Waverley's tomb can be found in the churchyard, which contains a good number of interesting old stones.

At least two old windows have been unblocked in recent years, including a Saxon one in the north wall of the nave. This section of the nave may have been the remains of the old building that the present church was built around. The church and the priest's house, which forms part of the boundary wall, are partially of flint, which reflects the nearness of the sea shore with its abundance of this building material. Close to the church are the ruins of an ancient manor house which may be the site of one of Alfred the Great's royal lodges.

EASTBOURNE *St Mary the Virgin* OSSA 184

🏛 🏛 ☆☆☆

Built using Caen stone in the late twelfth century, and enlarged substantially using greensand stone in the fourteenth, this large church sits on a slope leading down to the Bourne Stream. The nineteenth century restoration was kind to the ancient building and much remains intact. The Norman style chancel arch is second to none with its deeply cut double chevron design, and it dominates the older end of the nave. Close to it are the marks of the former rood loft and beam and high on the wall is a very rare rood piscina, which served an altar in the loft. The only entrance to the loft now is from the north side.

The nave pillars of Caen stone are alternately round and oblong with ornate capitals, and the later ones at the west end added in the fourteenth century, along with the Greensand stone tower and font, clearly show the difference in style from the earlier ones. The fourteenth century parclose screens of the chancel are of particular note and the northern one incorporates the much older rood screen door.

Facing the south door and greeting you as you enter is a carved head springing from an arch. This may well be a self-portrait of the master mason — it being a common practice for the master to work his likeness into the fabric of the church. There are six other heads to be found in the church, but these are more of a caricature nature.

In the chancel is the entrance to a rare medieval vestry and even rarer treasury, one of only two in Sussex. This is evidence of the vestry's original use as administrative office of the parish. Memorials abound and the wall-hanging monuments are the best in the county. People of note buried here include Thomas Mortimer, inventor of the horizontal windmill, and the MP and engineer Davies (Giddy) Gilbert.

The north door leads to a cloister which in turn leads to a fifteenth century parsonage. In the churchyard is an ancient Celtic cross brought from Cornwall by Davies Gilbert, and the old village cross now converted into a sundial.

WILLINGDON *St Mary the Virgin* OSSA 173 🏛🏛 ✰✰

The thirteenth century tower is all that remains of the original church that must have stood where the north aisle is now. This means that the tower stands a little behind the present church and very nearly separate from it. The nave we see today must have been a structure of some sort (perhaps a priest's house) before it was enlarged into the nave in the fourteenth century, as the gable and doorway of a smaller building can be clearly seen from the east end. The porch is the same date as the nave but the chancel was added about sixty years later. Just left of the porch a large consecration cross of flint can be seen built into a buttress. Some old gravestones have been built into the north tower wall but the most interesting item in the churchyard is a medieval stone coffin. The lids of these are rare enough (there is one inside the church in the chapel) but the coffins are almost unknown. This one seems to have survived only because it was used by a local farm as a cattle trough.

Inside the church there was extensive rebuilding in 1946 following major damage from two flying bombs in the Second World War. The stained glass is almost all of this date and is of some interest; the church guide gives detailed descriptions of all the windows.

The fourteenth century Ratton Chapel was adopted by the Parker family in the sixteenth century and has some good memorials, the best of which is that of Nicholas Parker, 1546-1619. The glass in the east window of the chapel survived the bombs and is seventeenth century. The rood beam in the chancel is modern but gives a good idea of what this common medieval feature was like.

FOLKINGTON *St Peter* OSSA 172 ☆

olkington is one of the line of churches that are tucked in the lee of the coastal Downs behind Eastbourne. It was built in the thirteenth century on an ancient mound (as are many of the others) and retains original lancet windows both in the nave and chancel. The blocked north door is also thirteenth century but a little later than the rest. Two windows of a different style (Perpendicular) were added to the nave at the very beginning of the fifteenth century along with the bell turret which retains its original bell (c1400).

The inside is plain and airy, with no visible division between nave and chancel, although from the outside the separation is clear. There are several seventeenth century grave slabs set in the floor of the nave, some eighteenth century memorials on the walls and a modern carving of Christ by the Sussex artist John Skelton. The font dates from around 1450 and has interesting decorated arches, while in the nave some box pews have survived.

The stresses put on the walls by the tie beam and crown post roof have meant the addition of quite heavy buttresses on the outside, at some time in the past. The churchyard is quite small and the stones look a little random, but many of the older ones have been removed to the boundary wall which may account for this.

The church is reached via a narrow road that peters out completely at the church, but parking is easy at this dead end.

WILMINGTON *St Mary and St Peter* OSSA 171 ☆☆☆

Following the conquest in 1066 this area came into the hands of the Abbey of Grestain in Normandy, whose monks built a small priory at Wilmington. The purpose was more administrative than religious and probably the priory had no more than two or three monks at any one time. It was decided to build a church to serve both monks and local people, and at one time the church was connected to the priory by a cloister. The partly-ruined priory, now a private house, can be seen just behind the church.

A truly massive yew, with a girth in excess of 23ft, dominates the church and churchyard. It has been scientifically dated at more than 1,600 years old. It is possible that pagan Anglo-Saxons worshipped at this tree long before the first Christian monks built their church on ground already considered holy.

The north door is thought to be almost 700 years old. Much of the chancel and some of the nave are twelfth century. The thick walls are splayed at the windows to allow maximum light to enter via a narrow space. Although the rood screen has gone the rood beam is still in place just to the east of the chancel arch. In the north chapel is an interesting stained glass window depicting British butterflies, moths and bees. Windows are a strong point in this church. In the chancel large three-light windows and two low sanctus windows were added. These seem to have weakened the walls, which had to be thick to hold the Norman roof with its typical outward stresses, and buttresses were added.

The pulpit is a rare Jacobean one and although splendid it looks a little out of place in this basically Norman church.

TOWERS AND PORCHES

Ask anyone today to draw a quick sketch of a church and nine times out of ten it will have a tower; everyone associates towers with churches, but not so 1,000 years ago. Very rarely was a Saxon church built with a tower, although sometimes a church was built very close to an existing defensive tower which in time became part of the church. The round tower at Southease was almost certainly built for defence and may pre-date the church. By the end of the Saxon era in England important churches were having towers added, often an upward extension of the porch, but refuge and defence were still the reason. Part of the tower at East Dean is from this time, with good strong walls, three feet thick.

The church porch played a very important role in medieval times as a kind of link between the village and the church. The first village council meetings were held in the porch, probably with the priest acting as an adviser and clerk, as he was usually the only literate person in the village.

The Saxon tower at Jevington

Important local decisions were proclaimed from the porch and even to this day the porch still performs this roll, often containing a village notice board on which, among other things, all political election results must be displayed.

The other major function of the porch was weddings. All marriages were performed outside the church in the porch, usually by one of the happy couple's relatives. The couple would then enter the church and have the marriage blessed by the priest. Even today the porch is still used on some occasions in part of the marriage service.

Strangely, many Sussex porches contain very old woodwork (Ringmer is a good example) while the stonework has often been replaced. At Bishopstone the porch has Saxon origins, although at that time it was a *porticus,* or small chapel.

With the coming of the Normans, church tower building really got under way and their uses began to change. Defence was still a consideration; the tower at Rottingdean was certainly used as a refuge as late as the fourteenth century. The reddish colour of the stones and the cracks on the inside are signs of the tower being set on fire by French raiders. On that occasion the tower proved inadequate and the villagers inside were killed.

By the twelfth century towers were being added to existing churches and new churches were often being

Ninfield church's brick porch

built with towers, sometimes the tower forming the main part of the nave, as at Newhaven.

Bells started to find their way into towers by the thirteenth century. Originally there would have been only one, quite small, bell used mostly to mark certain parts of the mass and indicate the start of the service. By the late fourteenth century towers were becoming the norm and were usually quite short, very heavily built and only lightly roofed. Windows were being added and the main church entrance was most likely through the tower.

Towers were usually built very slightly separate from the church to allow the greater weight to settle into the ground without pulling the church down with it. The later join can often still be seen.

In Sussex in the fifteenth century the Pelham family enter the picture. This important and wealthy family, whose seat was near Laughton, were great church benefactors and their favourite gift was a tower. Perhaps ten or more Pelham towers can be found in Sussex, all in the same Perpendicular style and carrying the Pelham badge or arms on them somewhere. So well built were these towers that several survive at places where the rest of the church has been totally rebuilt.

Roofing towers has always been a problem and many different methods of keeping out the weather have been tried in England. In Sussex a short pyramidal cap has proved the best, although churches needing a higher profile have ended up with spires, the Sussex broach spire proving to be the most suitable. East Blatchington has a perfect example of a broach spire and South Malling a perfect Sussex cap. Medieval stone spires are rare but Sussex has three, the most notable being at Dallington and the oldest at Chiddingly.

Towers can be found in any part of the church except the east. At Battle the original tower was to the south-east but the furthest east today is probably at Newhaven, where the tower almost forms part of the chancel, as the existing apsel chancel is so small. At Alfriston the central tower is held up on huge pillars at the very centre of the building and at Willingdon the tower only touches the rest of the church in the far north-west corner.

Most towers have had buttresses added to keep them stable. Clasping buttresses usually look the best, protruding as they do from the corners. At Westfield there are so many buttresses that the tower is almost completely hidden.

Clocks are a relatively new addition, although some are quite old examples of the clock-makers skill. Most suit their churches very well, especially at

The clock on Rye parish church

Kingston and Rottingdean, while a few seem a little out of place. At Mountfield the clock looks as if it were made for a tower three times as big.

The church tower today still performs one important function that it always has — as a landmark and indication of where the church is. Many coastal churches appeared on Royal Navy charts as important reference points, and countless land travellers both past and present have found their way by tracking the church tower. In fact, without towers to guide me, this book would have taken considerably longer to write.

WESTHAM *St Mary the Virgin* OSSA 175

t Mary's was one of the first, if not *the* first, church to be built in England following the conquest in 1066. It is even closer to the boundary wall of Pevensey castle on the west side than Pevensey's St Nicolas is on the east side. This proximity to the castle has not protected the church over the years; in fact quite the reverse, for every time the castle has been attacked the church, being outside the wall, was the first thing to be destroyed.

Of the original Norman church only the south wall with string course, three round-headed windows and part of the south transept remain. The chancel is for the most part fourteenth century and from the fifteenth century the solid green sandstone and flint west tower, porch and vestry survive.

Whether the Victorians thought the church had suffered enough we can't say, but they seem to have left it pretty much alone in the nineteenth century and quite a lot of interesting fifteenth century furnishings still exist. The font, wooden screens (chancel and chapel) and stained glass in the lights of the east window are all from this period. On the north and east sides the windows are almost all in the Perpendicular style.

Although modern, the rood loft is worth a look as it gives some idea of what this feature, which was common in medieval times, was like. The churchyard is well kept to the north and less so on the more interesting south side and contains a communal plague grave from the seventeenth century. The boundary wall is cut by an ancient stone country stile at the castle end, probably to allow access while keeping sheep in and cows out.

PEVENSEY *St Nicolas* OSSA 175 🏛🏛 ⭐⭐

ere at Pevensey there was once a major defensive neck of land protecting the natural harbour on the land side. The Romans built a stone fort here (the 'ey' in Pevensey was a Roman term for island) which was enlarged by the Normans who came ashore at Pevensey in 1066. The church stands close to the castle's east wall, and is just a half mile from another Norman church at Westham.

Apart from a small part of the twelfth century far western end of the chancel the earliest parts remaining today are the thirteenth century nave, chancel and lower tower. The upper tower and the porch came with the restoration work done in the nineteenth century.

Inside the Early English period prevails and the sharp pointed arches of the aisles and chancel arch are typical of this style. The lancet windows have almost all survived with three large ones at the east end. The chancel roof is a fine example of its type and blends well with the tall pointed chancel arch. There are two fonts, one modern, one ancient, and a fine early seventeenth century alabaster memorial in the north aisle.

The old stone doorframe contains many scratches thought to be crusader crosses. These were crudely carved by men waiting to leave the port to fight in the crusades. The custom was to cut the down stroke of the cross before leaving and add the cross piece to give thanks on your return. Some have no cross piece, which tells its own story. The church dedication to St Nicolas may also have crusader connections, as this saint was then a popular religious cult.

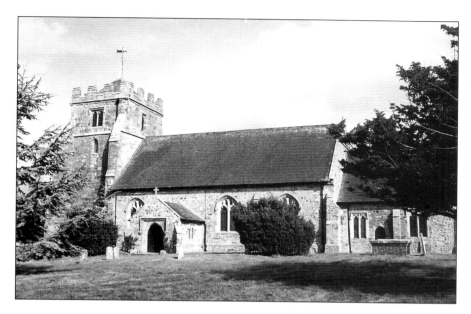

HOOE *St Oswald* OSSA 155 🏛 🍁

Most of the church we see today is the result of a fifteenth century rebuild. Only the thirteenth century north chapel survives from an earlier church, although the Saxon dedication to St Oswald hints of a much older church on the site. There are some nice, but badly worn carved heads on the south doorway, and on some of the windows forming the label stops. More fifteenth century carving around the doorway is in the form of leaves and flowers, possibly a rose.

Inside the building signs of the rood loft are the blocked doorways that led to it and the corbels that were part of its supports. The large blocked north doorway now forms a recess. The early twelfth century font is of Sussex marble and has the four corner supports often seen on Norman fonts in Sussex. There is an ancient dugout chest of English oak with metal bands. Reset in the East window are some fragments of medieval stained glass depicting the Coronation of the Virgin.

The graveyard is not over-populated and contains some interesting stones and chest tombs. The setting is quite remote, the church being reached via a long narrow lane. The blocked north door and the church's present lonely position may mean that the village was closer in the past and was moved to its present site, perhaps at the time of the plague.

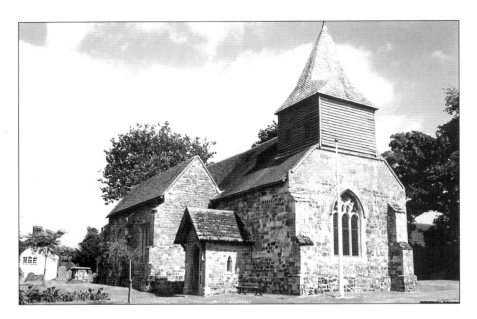

WARTLING *St Mary Magdalene* OSSA 154

he church is built on high ground and in Saxon times would have been close to the sea. The Domesday Book shows the village to have been a prosperous one and, although no church is mentioned, there was a chapel and this is thought to have stood on the site of the present church.

The earliest remaining parts of the present church are the north and south chancel walls and a small part of the western end of the nave, which are thirteenth century. The north aisle was added in the fourteenth and the south in the fifteenth centuries. The original door was probably the south porch and this was still in use in 1736 when it was rebuilt. In Victorian times a north porch was built using a fifteenth century doorway, which may have come from another church or nearby building. On the outside of the south wall can be seen a Pelham buckle and a Catherine wheel. Sir John Pelham's daughter Katherine died in 1459, and the south aisle may have been built in her memory and dedicated to St Catherine.

Inside, the church retains a rare full set of box pews. With their heating pipes lacing along the footings these are certainly snugger in winter than their modern counterparts, but not as comfortable. Above the fourteenth century chancel arch are the arms of George II and under the belfry are displayed the only known iron grave decorations made by Harmer, the famous maker of terracotta grave plaques. The modern elm lectern in the shape of a heron, a stunning and unique design, is fitting as there have been heronries here since the 1650s.

HERSTMONCEUX *All Saints* OSSA 131   🏛 🍁 ☆☆

lthough closer to the castle of the same name than the village, the church pre-dates the former by some centuries, and there is evidence that the village moved from a closer vicinity following the plague. Although on the site of a pre-conquest church, the oldest parts now remaining are late twelfth century (tower and north west wall) with most of the remainder being added over the next 200 years — the coming of the castle adding to these changes.

View this church from every direction and note the vast differences, the south aspect being the oddest, looking very much like a large house. Look too for Harmer terracottas in the churchyard and the large mounting block by the gate.

This is perhaps the only church in the county where the tower forms part of the west end of the nave. Inside, some fifteenth century glass can be seen in the chapel and there is a nice brass of Sir William Fiennes, but the main treasure is the Dacre tomb. On this lie the effigies of Thomas Dacre (1470-1533) and his son in full armour with a large canopy above in Caen stone. The north side of the tomb shows some weather wear and is thought to have formed part of the outside wall of the church until the chapel was added as protection. This chapel is built of brick and is one of the earliest uses of the material in church building in Sussex.

HELLINGLY *St Peter and St Paul* OSSA 129

Hellingly sits in a particularly picturesque setting, with a row of cottages forming part of the boundary wall. The churchyard is round, which is quite rare (only about three in Sussex) and this is usually an indication of Saxon beginnings.

The round-headed windows in the chancel are twelfth century and their shaft decoration and frieze work survived the extensive Victorian restoration of the interior. The other windows in the chancel are thirteenth century lancets.

It is interesting to look closely at the material used in the building of the chancel. Many broken carved blocks can be seen used as simple wall filling; these must have come from some earlier building on or very near the site. The original nave walls disappeared in the fourteenth century when the arcades were added; the windows in these arcades are particularly good.

The rectangular tower is quite new, being nineteenth century. There are doors in the north, south and west walls and although the south is the one used today it is worth taking a look at the small north porch with its lead memorial to the churchwardens of 1685.

The churchyard is quite sparsely populated but there are three stones with Harmer terracotta plaques. It always amazes me to see the pristine condition of these decorative plaques. Quite often the gravestone is worn smooth while the terracotta is as good as new. They say the technique died with Harmer. A good number of very old stones have been moved to the east boundary wall.

JOHN FULLER

Of all the many colourful and interesting people connected with East Sussex churches over the centuries surely John Fuller must rate a small chapter. The Fullers were one of the great ironmaster families of Sussex. In the sixteenth and seventeenth centuries they gained great wealth, with which they bought an estate at Brightling in 1698. Constantly expanded and improved, this estate passed to John Fuller in the late 1700s. John, a one-time Member of Parliament, was a great patron of the arts and sciences — the artist Turner often stayed and painted at the estate. Whole books could, and indeed have been written about John Fuller's eccentric lifestyle, but as this is a book about churches, we will look at his eccentricities in that direction.

'Mad Jack' as he was called by some — 'Honest Jack' by others — loved to build follies. Many can be found around Brightling and one of the most interesting is in the churchyard. Twenty-four years before his death Fuller decided to build his tomb in the form of a 28ft high pyramid made of sandstone blocks. In a way typical of Fuller he gained permission to use this large piece of land by agreeing with the rector to build a new inn some way along the road to replace the inn opposite the church, which was proving more popular with the villagers than the church. This inn, the Fullers Arms, still stands.

Another of his follies with church connections is Fuller's Point, also known as the Sugar Loaf. This church spire-shaped construction, standing all alone in a field, is indeed just that. One day while walking with a friend Fuller made a

'Mad Jack' Fuller's tomb at Brightling

wager that he could see the spire of Dallington church from his house, but when he arrived home he found he could not. To win the bet he quickly had a copy of the spire built in a field beyond some trees, at a spot where it could be seen from the house.

A great benefactor of the church, Fuller made many improvements to Thomas à Becket at Brightling, the most interesting being the barrel organ he commissioned in 1820. This is the biggest in England and is in full working order. Another gift to the church, but one perhaps not given with such good grace, was of nine bassoons which he sent to the church choir after complaining about their singing.

Of all the stories told about Mad Jack Fuller the most intriguing is about his burial. It is said he is buried in his pyramid sitting in a chair dressed in his best clothes, powdered wig and top hat, holding a bottle of claret in one hand and a pipe in the other. Church sources say this is not true and that he is buried under a simple slab in the floor. Interestingly, the door to the tomb, with its tiny barred window, was bricked up some years ago to prevent anyone entering or even seeing in. It seems quite clear to me which of the two burial options Mad Jack would have preferred.

The church at Brightling

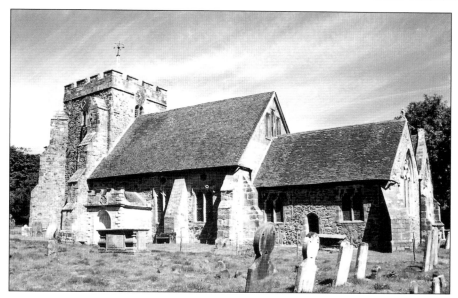

BRIGHTLING *St Thomas à Becket* OSSA 85 🏛 🍁 ☆

his basically thirteenth century church has benefited from two or three rich benefactors over the centuries, resulting in a quite large parish church that retains its compact shape. Large buttresses were added to the tower in the fourteenth century presumably to support the heavy battlements, which were added at the same time. Two large decorated windows at the east end, with reticulated tracery, overpower the lancet windows which also look east from high up on the nave.

The interior contains some good brasses and the remains of wall paintings, some of which date from the fourteenth century, as do a few fragments of glass in one window. One quite rare feature is the wooden gallery, once a common way of increasing the capacity without rebuilding; very few survived the Victorian era. This one was donated by the most famous of Sussex's iron masters, Jack Fuller, who also gave the barrel organ, which can be seen in the gallery.

The church sits up high in the village and the churchyard contains some interesting iron grave markers, as well as Fuller's 25ft pyramid tomb, all reminders of the iron industry that flourished here 200 years ago.

CATSFIELD *St Laurence* OSSA 133 🏛🏛 🍁 ☆☆

atsfield is a very old village, in fact the very name may derive from the Saxon *Catti* tribe and there has certainly been a church here since early times. The present early Norman church probably contains parts of a pre-conquest church and stands next to the old manor house, just as it did when Domesday described it as 'a small church to serve the manor house'.

The nave and tower were rebuilt in the twelfth century, perhaps with defence in mind for even the nave wall is nearly 4ft thick. Buttresses were built on to the tower in the fifteenth century, when bells and a spire were added. The bells are quite impressive and of some historic interest, but sadly are unusable except for one service bell also used by the nineteenth century clock.

The spire, although re-shingled many times, still has its original fifteenth century frame. In the chancel is a unique holy water stoup built inside a hollowed out pillar and usable from two sides. In the north wall behind the organ is a very old unmarked tomb with a six foot slab top. Beneath the floor members of the Ashburnham family are buried, as well as at least one of that famous family of Sussex church benefactors, the Pelhams.

The yews in the churchyard are mere youngsters by Sussex churchyard standards at less than 200 years, but until 1960 there was a massive oak dating from the time of conquest, with a girth of 48ft. Many churchyards have military markers but two here are of particular interest as the two men actually died on active service in the area, on May 6, 1944, trying to defuse one of the many unexploded flying bombs that fell in the area.

BEXHILL *St Peter* OSSA 157 ☆☆☆

A charter set out by King Offa records the exact date when it was decided to build a church on this site. It was August 15, 772. The dimensions are also known: 40ft long, 20ft wide starting at what is now the tower step.

A small part of the Saxon church remains today high above the two western-most bays of the aisle arches which were cut through the Saxon walls. Also from the Saxon church is a beautifully carved 8th century reliquary lid, now on show in a glass case. It was found under the nave floor and, interestingly, it is made of a stone found only in the north of England. Offa was a northern king — did he send it south with his charter 1,200 years ago?

In 1090 the Normans enlarged the church and from that date the large tower (minus its Perpendicular top section) and the three western-most sets of nave pillars remain. The pillars are perhaps of slightly differing dates as they vary in style. The tower window and buttress were added in the fifteenth century. The window in the north aisle contains thirteenth and fifteenth century glass which started life in the church, fell into private hands in 1750 and was reinstated on St Peter's day, 1921.

The northern chapel, known as the chantry, was built in 1425 and used as a school in 1597. The glass from its fifteenth century window was removed and used elsewhere in the church when the organ room blocked the light. In the Lady Chapel the old barrel organ, which saw service until 1881, is on display. Much of the thirteenth century chancel was lost during the restoration of 1878, which is also when the present font (a copy of the ancient one) was installed.

NINFIELD *St Mary the Virgin* OSSA 133 🍁🍁🍁 ☆

here was certainly a Saxon church on this spot long before the conquest, and three large doorway stones now built into the north wall are all that remain. Much of the nave is thirteenth century, and the chancel seventeenth, but extensive Victorian restoration of the worst kind destroyed or covered up much of the old church. Happily some features have been uncovered in the last eighty years; these include the seventeenth century musician's gallery and the very early fourteenth century roof beams and crown posts, both boarded up in 1885.

There is a nice Jacobean priest's prayer desk and a rare royal coat of arms of James I; few royal arms of pre-Cromwellian times survived and this is a good one. The clock housed in the clapboard bell turret was built in 1897 and the moving parts can be seen through glass doors in the nave. Its extremely loud tick resounds through the church. The one surviving bell, dated 1395, still sounds the hours and calls the congregation to the services.

In the churchyard the yew tree may pre-date even the Saxon church, and an area of the graveyard has been left wild, encouraging birds and wildflowers to take advantage of the sanctuary within the boundary wall. Being so high up the view over the Pevensey levels, from the east side of the boundary wall, is extensive. It is worth reflecting that the priest of St Mary, looking out from this spot in the autumn of 1066, over what was then a large natural harbour, would have been one of the first people in England to see the arrival of the Conqueror's fleet.

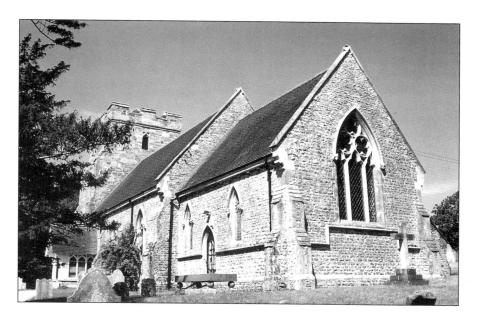

CROWHURST *St George* OSSA 134 ☆

here has certainly been a church on this site for 1,000 years, but apart from the tower the present building is nineteenth century. The church has pleasing lines and fits well into the surrounding vista. The windows are mostly Perpendicular in design, as is the impressive west door. The tower, built like so many others in the area by the Pelham family, in the fifteenth century, has the Pelham buckle as label stops on the doorway.

The rest of the church that went with this tower seems to have gone without repair from its building *c*1450 until 1794 when, following a poor attempt to save the original building in 1729, nothing could be done but rebuild the nave and much of the chancel.

In the nineteenth century the parish population had more than doubled and the chancel was rebuilt to its original size and a new nave and sanctuary were built. The tower, with its huge buttress and embattled parapet, remained untouched throughout.

The east window was badly damaged by a flying bomb in the Second World War, and has been replaced, giving more light to the chancel. There are the remains of a yew tree in the churchyard thought to have been more than 1,000 years old and still living in 1986. Its girth was measured at 42ft in 1938. There are many short, solid gravestones in the churchyard, typical of those found on the Kent side of East Sussex.

HOLLINGTON *St Leonard* OSSA 135 🏛 🍁 🍁 ☆

This has always been known as 'the church in the wood', and that is certainly still the case for, although Hastings has encroached, the church still stands deep in a wood, much as the first building did in Saxon times. The oldest remaining visible part of the church is the west wall below the tower, which is thirteenth century. Examination of the filling of the original walls during the 1865 rebuilding showed them to have been made of bluestone and sandstone.

For once we must thank the Victorians for the work done in 1865, for the building was in such bad condition that demolition was the only other alternative to rebuilding. So secluded is the church that electricity was not laid on until 1977. Until then the church was lit by candles and, to this day, all services are candlelit. Of the many candelabras the most interesting is the large brass one midway down the aisle, which was brought from a Russian church during the Crimean War.

There is one very old tie beam, much supported, and one very old bell in the tower. The bell is dated at 1380 and because of wear is now fixed in position and chimed rather than rung. The marble pulpit dates from the rebuilding, and the oldest of the windows now look into the vestry rather than outside.

The churchyard is enormous and contains a very interesting mix of memorials spanning nearly 350 years. There are five military stones, mostly from World War One. The most striking memorial is the massive 'broken pillar' with a carving of the occupier's head with a death's scythe laid across him.

MOUNTFIELD *All Saints* OSSA 87

he church at Mountfield is quite rare in that the chancel, nave and tower all date from the same century (twelfth), although the tower was added a few years after the rest. The tower is very short, not reaching the height of the nave roof, indicating that it may have been reduced in height at some time, perhaps when the broach spire was added; it supports a huge clock far too large for the tower.

The south porch is fourteenth century and retains some very old timbers. Inside is a Norman font, with later carvings added, and some fine medieval wall paintings, some of which date from the thirteenth century, as do the lancet windows and squints.

Although approached through a wooded area the views from the well-kept churchyard are quite spectacular and it contains some interesting stones, including two with Harmer terracottas. The most notable gravestone, and perhaps the saddest, is a naval marker for V A Fennell, who could have been in the navy for only a few weeks for he was at HMS *Ganges,* a land-based training ship. His rank was 'Boy 2nd class' (the lowest possible rank) and he was only fifteen years old when he died in 1919.

BATTLE *St Mary the Virgin* OSSA 12 🏛🏛 ☆☆

Nothing remains of the town's first, twelfth century church, whose nave followed the lines of the six eastern-most pillars of the present nave, and whose chancel extended a quarter of the way into the current chancel. The first tower stood where the present St Catherine's Chapel is situated, and the outline of the arch can still be seen.

Perhaps the best feature of the present church is the thirteenth century Romanesque nave, the western part of which is a slightly later addition. The main entrance is through the west door of the fifteenth century tower, built at the same time as the north aisle was added and most of the outside walls were refaced. A modern Sussex oak screen opening into the nave now marks the earlier west door.

The font is almost 900 years old and the medieval cover is the oldest in Sussex. The medieval wall paintings feature a series of panels depicting the life story of St Margaret of Antioch. These are a good example of the teaching purpose paintings had in medieval times. In about 1230 the chancel was rebuilt and with very few alterations is much the same today.

In the St Catherine chapel crusader crosses have been carved into a pillar behind the Dean's stall, along with the slits where they blunted their swords on their return from the Holy Land.

Memorials include the *c*1550 coloured, alabaster tomb of Sir Anthony Browne and his wife, and a modern stained glass window commemorating the English and Norman soldiers who fell at the Battle of Hastings in 1066.

PENHURST *St Michael the Archangel* OSSA 110

The church, manor house and farm stand together in a beautiful setting, much as they have since the fourteenth century. The nave and its windows are original, with a short solid tower with unusual raised cap being added some 100 years later.

The tower has a particularly good doorway and window. The doorway is still used, as is the south porch, which still retains some medieval woodwork. On show inside the tower is a carved, very rare mason's stone, a sort of on-site builders plan. On the north side of the nave is a hagioscope, or squint, which gives a clear view of the main altar from a previous side altar.

For those not sure of the difference between a crown post and a wagon roof, both are on show here, the former in the nave, the latter in the chancel.

The church was in a very dilapidated state in the nineteenth century when major restoration took place. In a move completely out of character the Victorians not only left the original features unchanged, but actually added beautiful box pews, a feature they were diligently throwing out everywhere else.

The north chapel is seventeenth century and formerly included a private pew for the local gentry. The exceptional furnishings, which also survived the Victorian changes, include a fifteenth century screen between nave and chancel, a seventeenth century communion rail and a Jacobean pulpit and reading desk.

The church and churchyard are particularly well kept and are in as beautiful a setting as you are likely to see anywhere in England.

WHATLINGTON *St Mary Magdalene* OSSA 88

There was almost certainly a Saxon church here but it was probably totally destroyed in 1066 when the village is described in the Domesday Book as being 'laid waste' by the Norman army. A Norman chapel was built in the twelfth century but the present building is basically thirteenth. The lancets, low side window and main east window all date from this period as do the clasping buttress on the nave walls. The south wall of the nave has four windows, all of which are slightly different and look a little odd.

The nave and chancel are of different widths, but the same height, and internally there is no division. The font is a typical thirteenth century square heavy model and nearby is an early seventeenth century brass. The carved pulpit was exhibited at the Great Exposition of 1851, which means it was the height of fashion then, but is perhaps a little over the top by modern tastes.

In the nineteenth century the tower and vestry, with its out-of-place apsel bulge, were added, and both add little to the appearance. Viewed from the south west, it is still possible to visualise the simple clean lines of the old two-cell church with its west doorway.

The churchyard contains a few interesting stones, including one military marker, but the most interesting outdoor feature is the row of trees running north-south then turning east. Early drawings and paintings of churches show very few trees other than the oaks and yews that often pre-date the church. The planting of trees in churchyards seems to have coincided with the great landscape garden boom of the eighteenth century.

ASHBURNHAM *St Peter* OSSA 110 🏛 ✬

The church stands next to Ashburnham Place formerly the home of the Earls of Ashburnham and now the Christian Conference Centre. The church was completely rebuilt in 1665 by John Ashburnham, with the exception of the fifteenth century Pelham tower. There is little of interest on the outside but a great deal inside, where the appearance is quite stark, especially in the chapels. The considerable ironwork, and bright clear light from the seventeenth century windows add to this. The ironwork, in the form of screens and railings, is unique and was made at Ashburnham forge — once famous throughout the south of England for its wrought iron work.

The memorials are dominated by two massive marble tomb chests with canopies. Both built between 1670 and 1680 yet are totally different in style. The tomb of William Ashburnham (d1675) is considered the best of is kind in Sussex. The box pews are original but have been lowered at some time. There are interesting commandment and prayer boards as well as some nice funeral hatchments.

The gallery at the west end was formerly the private pew of the Ashburnhams and now houses the organ. It is reached by a good example of a seventeenth century domestic staircase. The sixteenth century font is unusually rounded and smooth and is much smaller than the twelfth to fourteenth century fonts, as by this time total immersion in the font was no longer the custom. The three-sided communion rail is also very rare.

HASTINGS *All Saints* OSSA 160   🏛 🍁 ☆☆

All Saints sits on high sloping ground in the old town, a little east of modern Hastings. The first church on the site was Norman and probably served the settlement that grew up in the area after the old Saxon town was destroyed following the battle in 1066. Often the scene of French raids, the church was burnt twice — the second time in 1377, causing its total destruction.

It was rebuilt on a grand scale in the Perpendicular style in the early fifteenth century and the building is impressive and of good proportions. The inside is, if anything, even more impressive with its barrel roof which has no divide between nave and chancel, giving the impression of great length. The arches are worthyof note, particularly that leading from the nave to the tower with its fluted hexagonal columns. A plain octagonal font, contemporary with the church, is still in regular use.

There are the remains of a fifteenth century Doom painting above the chancel arch and near the blocked north doorway can be seen the Royal Arms of George II. In addition, six funeral hatchments with the arms of the deceased can be seen high up on the nave walls. The rather overgrown churchyard has some interesting stones — one for a nine-year-old boy killed by a mule he kept teasing, and another to Joe Swaine, a smuggler shot by a revenue man in 1821.

CHURCH EXTERIORS

When we approach an ancient church the impression is that we are looking at a building that hasn't changed in hundreds of years. In fact just the opposite is true of all ancient churches. Since their earliest times each church has changed continually. It is commonplace for a church to have been enlarged then made smaller then enlarged again, had a tower added or one removed, had two or three doors and/or windows added, while others have been blocked up, windows and stained glass moved and even the exterior finish changed. Only in the last 100 years has the process slowed, with restoration rather than change being the order of the day.

Scratch dial at Litlington

Saxon and Norman churches were, in the main, two-cell churches consisting of nave and chancel. Towers were rare, the exterior was usually rendered with plaster and the roof thatched or covered with stone slabs. All of these conditions still exist but rarely, if ever, all in the same church. Tarring Neville gives a good idea of what a rendered exterior would have been like, as does Chalvington which is pretty much still a two-cell church but with a sixteenth century bell turret and an added porch. At Southease the original large chancel has long disappeared with part of the nave becoming the present chancel.

Mounting block, Berwick

Early churches would have had one door, often in the west wall. A little later the north wall became favourite for the main door, as it seems to be today. As more ceremony became part of services other doors were added to allow for processions and for priests to enter and exit. Many of the priest doors have been blocked, but Beddingham still retains a good example.

Do not be in too much of a hurry to enter a church for its real history is in the fabric of the building. In a typical Norman church perhaps only one Norman wall remains, but this one wall can have so much to tell us. It is often quite clear where the builders stopped work for the winter months then restarted in

the spring. A layer of mortar was left to protect the top of an unfinished wall and another added at the re-start in the spring, and in places this clearly shows.

The size of the original church can sometimes be determined from a small piece of original wall or its corners. At St Mary, Westham, which proclaims itself 'the first church built by the Normans' only one small area is original, which is the price paid for building a church so close to a castle that has been besieged at least twice.

Arlington church was described in an eighteenth century account as being 'totally in ruins', a far cry from the beautiful and, to all intents and purposes, original church and churchyard to be seen today. Norman churches have thicker, heavier walls than the earlier Saxon ones so you are more likely to see a more complete Norman church than a Saxon one.

Flying buttress, Winchelsea

The lawn mowers of Ashburnham churchyard

Porch and Saxon window, Arlington

Like the churchyard the building can tell us much of the village history; as the village grew so the church would have been enlarged, the addition of north and or south aisles on the inside often causing the demolition of ancient original walls on the outside. If the village became smaller, say after the plague or,as is often the case in Sussex, when the nearby river or even parts of the sea silted up, the church might be made smaller. At Iford the present north wall follows the line of an earlier north aisle and the arches can clearly be seen from the outside as part of the wall. Just the opposite has occurred at Herstmonceux where the beautiful Dacre tomb and effigies appear to have been situated outside the wall of the church and didn't have any protection from the elements until their present chapel was added.

Many early churches, especially Norman churches, had an apse, usually a semi-circular extension to the chancel. These have almost all been demolished with only five remaining in Sussex, good examples being at St Cosmas and St Damian, Keymer, and St Michael, Newhaven where the church's hill-side position seems to have saved it. In some cases a village may have moved a short distance and as the main door of a church was often placed facing the village a new door would be added to face the village once again. If a church were lucky enough to gain the attention of a rich benefactor, additions both inside and outside could be extensive. The Pelham family built extensions to quite a few Sussex churches, usually towers — notably at Laughton and Ripe.

So take a good look at the outside, walk all the way round the church before going in. Careful observation of the exterior can often reveal a surprising amount of what to expect on the inside.

WADHURST *St Peter and St Paul* OSSA 30 🏛 ☆☆

Only the tower of the twelfth century church remains, all the rest having disappeared as the church of this very prosperous medieval parish grew between the thirteenth and eighteenth centuries. Most of the nave and chancel date from the fourteenth century, the notable porch with its room above being added in the fifteenth. The broach spire is 123ft tall and was built in the fourteenth century. It is clearly seen to be out of alignment, which is hardly surprising since, during the great storm of 1987, it was actually lifted by the wind but settled back into place. The weather vane is dated 1699.

The churchyard is large and well populated with stones almost as massive as the iron slabs inside the church. There are also eleven military grave markers, including what must surely be one of the rarest, a member of the Women's Royal Air Force, dated 1919. There are several Harmer terracottas, the most unusual of which is a painted one on a memorial inside the porch.

Inside, the church has memorials of all kinds, including the huge iron grave slabs for which the church is nationally famous. There are more than thirty of these, mostly seventeenth century, and made for the great iron masters. All are in good condition but the best are to be found in the chancel.

Next to the thirteenth century font is the door to the parvise, or upper room to the porch. To the left of the font is a window containing glass designed by pre-Raphaelite artist Edward Burne-Jones and made by William Morris. It depicts Christ among the children. A window at the east end of the south aisle is in memory of the 114 men of the parish who died in the 1914-18 war.

TICEHURST *St Mary the Virgin* OSSA 31 🍁 ☆☆

The size of this church reflects the prosperity of the area due to the iron industry, which first flourished in the fourteenth century when most of the present church was built. The west tower has had a stair turret and shingle spire added and contains a large Perpendicular window with original tracery above the west door.

The large churchyard is sparsely populated on the north side, a condition common in ancient times when the north side was considered the dark side. There are, however, some very old stones to be found, especially on the south side, where a very early stone dated 1685 can still be read in full.

Inside, the large size is emphasised by the huge tower arch, arcades to north and south aisles and the chapels. The windows and part of the walls in this area are from a smaller thirteenth century church. The clerestory and east window are Victorian, but a rare piece of fifteenth century glass has been mounted in the north sanctuary. It is from a 'doom' and shows naked people in a cart being pulled by devils. One of the people wears a crown and another a mitre, perhaps to show that all are considered equal when penance is due.

The ornate sixteenth century font cover is of interest, as are the rare Victorian bier and eighteenth century prayer boards, both well preserved. The fine state of preservation of the church, and especially the tower, allows for a full set of bells, which are still in regular use.

WALDRON *All Saints* OSSA 80 🏛 🍁 ☆☆

uilt in the Early English style of the thirteenth century, this large village church has seen many changes, although the basic structure of nave, chancel and tower are original. The large east window is later and is flanked by two blocked lancet predecessors.

The church is typical of those in the old iron founding area in showing signs of many rich benefactors from the fifteenth to seventeenth centuries. The tower has benefited from many of these additions, including a stair turret, battlements and a clock.

Inside there are many memorials spread around the building including some nice seventeenth century ledger slabs and a large marble monument to John Fuller (see page 75), one of the well-known Sussex family of ironmasters. The altar slab now used in the north chapel is very rare being of pre-Reformation date. It was found during Victorian restoration and was probably the original main altar prior to the sixteenth century changes.

The churchyard is wooded and pleasing to the eye; a little searching will reveal some wooden graveboards and Harmer terracottas.

ETCHINGHAM *The Assumption of Blessed Mary and St Nicolas*
OSSA 44   🏛🏛🏛   ☆☆

Built in the fourteenth century (1366-69) Etchingham church has changed very little. Probably designed by a French architect, it is entirely of the Decorated period. The only small changes of note are the small nineteenth century vestry (now a boiler room) to the north of the chancel, and the removal of a much earlier chapel just to the east of it.

The church has a central tower with a large, almost square nave, and much narrower chancel. The church was built on the site of a previous one by Sir William de Echyngham, who is buried in the chancel where he has an impressive memorial. Also in the chancel, and of the fourteenth century, are twelve choir stalls with carved misericords, two of which are of a fox preaching to a congregation of geese.

To the side of the north door is an ancient crude mass dial and on the top of the low tower what may be the oldest weathervane still in use in the country. It takes the form of the Etchingham coat of arms and is still on its original support.

The church vaults were filled with concrete in 1937when considerable subsidence occurred, and it was at this time that the braces on the upper tower were added. The east window of the north transept contains all that remains of the original fourteenth century stained glass which was collected from various parts of the church and inserted there in 1931. The ancient oak chest is probably a churchwarden's as it has only two locks; a parish chest would have had three. The stone altar is modern, probably very similar to the original altar.

OLD HEATHFIELD *All Saints* OSSA 82 🏛🏛 ✰✰

Externally the church at Old Heathfield looks much as it did in the fourteenth century. Nave, chancel, tower, aisles and even the clerestory are all original. The construction is of sandstone,with the exception of the tower which is made of chalk faced with sandstone.

The parish is large today but was even larger in the past. In 1745 a singing gallery was added, and in 1820 north and south side galleries were built, bringing the seating up to 500. The church census of 1851 shows an average attendance of 180 in the morning, 300 in the evening. Unfortunately all three galleries were removed in the extensive Victorian restoration of the 1890s.

There is a large squint in one aisle and a monk's seat now used as an altar in the north aisle. The window in the north aisle shows former Heathfield vicar Robert Hunt celebrating the first communion in Jamestown USA in 1607. He went as chaplain to a settlement there in 1606 and there is a monument on the James River commemorating the event.

The funeral hatchments are for the Blunts (south side) and Lord Heathfield (north side); the royal arms are George III.

An Elizabethan oak alms box has survived as has the eighteenth century parish chest which can be seen in the tower. Jonathan Harmer, whose terracotta plaques decorate many gravestones in Sussex, had his factory in Heathfield and the churchyard and church wall have some good examples. Near the boundary wall one adorns a gravestone of one of the Harmer family.

Chancel arch at Peasmarsh

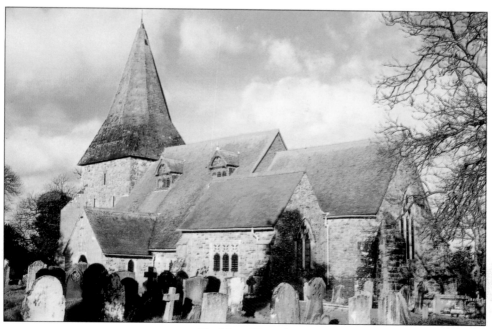

Beckley Church

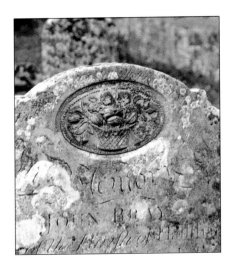

A Harmer terracotta

Thomas Selwyn's memorial at Friston

Telscombe

Stones with stylised skull motif, Guestling

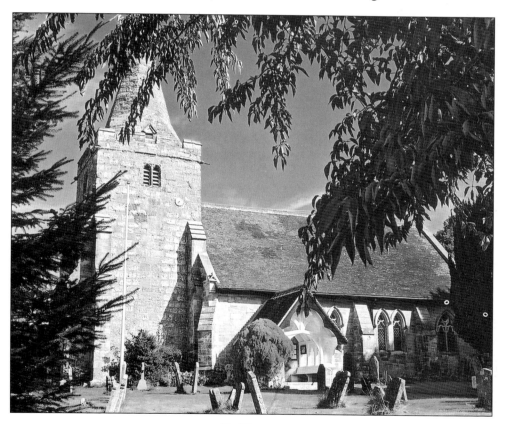

Dallington

Rye church: above, the water tower in the churchyard; right, the south transept window; below, the churchyard

100

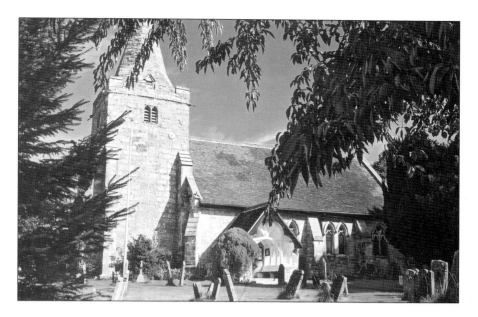

DALLINGTON *St Giles* OSSA 84

ictorian restoration has much to answer for in the loss of so many ancient features, and no more so than at Dallington where all of the old church, except the fifteenth century Pelham tower, was demolished. As usual the tower contains recognition of the Pelhams, this time the family badge and arms on the parapet wall.

The spire is the most notable feature of the church, being one of only three medieval stone spires in Sussex. It is also known for one of the Fuller follies (see Jack Fuller, page 75).

The font is almost certainly of the same date as the tower but practically everything else inside the church, including the memorials, was removed during the 1865 rebuilding. In recent years a few eighteenth century wall tablets were found in the tower and have been re-mounted on the north wall.

The churchyard is lightly wooded and very pleasing to the eye with some areas growing wild — offering a little sanctuary to birds, animals and insects. Some of the latter have been almost completely eradicated from the outside world by modern pesticides and farming techniques, and it is thought that some butterflies exist almost exclusively in churchyards where their natural habitat is protected by the boundary wall.

BURWASH *St Bartholomew* OSSA 62 🏛 ☆

The first stone church here was built about 1090 and of that church the tower still survives. The tower walls are more than three feet thick but the inside measurement is only eighteen feet square, giving a gloomy entrance followed by a bright airy interior. The chancel, aisles and porch were all rebuilt in 1856, the present chancel being a copy of the earlier one.

On the walls of the porch can be seen the original battlefield grave markers of some of the local men who died in the First World War. These were brought to the church with the help of Rudyard Kipling, who worshipped at the church, and who was involved with the War Graves Commission in 1919. On the south wall there is a memorial to Kipling's son, who was one of those killed.

The font is carved with Pelham buckles, suggesting that it was a gift of that generous family of church benefactors. The chancel arch is thirteenth century but sits on fourteenth century corbels. The north arcade is also thirteenth century but the south is earlier.

Among the many memorials are the earliest known iron graveslab, dated 1343, and to the left of the altar, a cross in memory of Cecil Cooper, who became Bishop of Korea in 1930, and who suffered great hardship at the hands of the Chinese communist forces.

The churchyard contains a couple of military graves and two stones with Harmer terracottas. Just outside the boundary wall is an interesting town war memorial that contains a light which is lit on the anniversary of each of those who gave their lives.

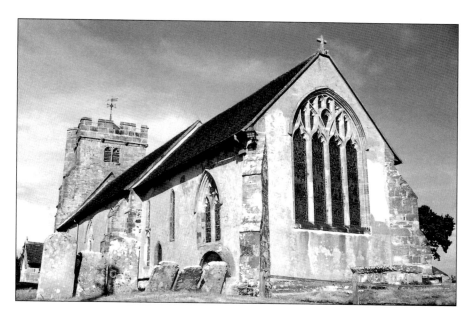

WARBLETON *St Mary* OSSA 83 🍁🍁 ☆☆☆

Warbleton sits high up with a pretty churchyard and extensive views across to the Downs. The churchyard contains some old stones, two with Harmer terracottas, and a memorial to Richard Woodman, one of the Protestants burnt at the stake in Lewes in 1557.

The building is a good example of several styles coming together in reasonable harmony, Perpendicular tower (with large carved heads protruding), Decorated nave and Early English chancel. Entry is through the south door, which is very unusual for a church door, being in two halves.

The inside is dominated by the squire's private pew, which stands high on legs and is reached by a stairway. Built in 1722, it perhaps gives an insight into the class structure of the time, for those sitting in it would be higher than everyone else, even the priest. Under the squire's pew is a thirteenth century iron bound parish chest with its obligatory three locks (one key for the priest and one for each churchwarden).

There are a few fragments of heraldic fifteenth century glass and evidence of several former side altars in their now obsolete piscina. One lancet window has been converted into a low side window, a practice common in Sussex. This one is quite high.

There are two outstanding monuments, the 1436 canopied brass to William Prestwyck, set in the floor, and the wall monument containing the bust of Sir John Lade (d1740). Unfortunately, this monument, perhaps the best of its kind anywhere, is hidden away behind the organ.

MAYFIELD *St Dunstan* OSSA 40 ☆☆

In the tenth century Dunstan, Saxon Archbishop of Canterbury and later St Dunstan, built wooden churches on all of his estates, including here at Mayfield. The first church was replaced by a Norman one that was all but destroyed by fire in 1389. Surviving from that building are the tower and a small fragment of the nave to the north west, with one lancet.

The church was rebuilt in the fifteenth century in the Perpendicular style with the final additions coming in the sixteenth, and it is from this time that the present dedication dates. The Tudor style clerestory windows are quite unusual as is the two-storey porch with vaulted ceiling. Just inside is a painted wall monument dated 1602 consisting of two kneeling people. Other monuments include several iron slabs and seventeenth century memorials. The font is also seventeenth century and clearly dated 1666. From the eighteenth century are the brass chandeliers and pulpit.

The church was struck by lightning in 1622 and the arcades may have been rebuilt during the repairs. There is some evidence of this at the eastern end where the arches are incomplete. The chancel arch is wooden and the area above is also wood as the arch could not support an infill of stone.

The churchyard stretches away in one direction, obviously extended as the village grew. Several stones have Harmer terracottas and there are three military stones. These official armed service stones are always interesting, many of the regiments are long gone and one can only guess what purpose some of them had. Here is one such stone to a man who served in the Labour Corps.

INTERIORS AND FURNISHINGS

The inside of a medieval church today is very different from how it was 400 years ago. To begin with there were no pews, in fact no seating at all other than a narrow stone bench along the walls for the use of the old or weak. The saying 'the weak go to the wall' comes from here. The congregation would have stood on an earth floor, with perhaps a couple of stone coffin lids protruding from it, and been virtually unable to see what was going on in the chancel, which was screened off. It is quite likely that the priests paid little attention to the congregation other than to allow them to be present in the building during the mass.

Very few written accounts survive of what services were like, but one detailed report paints a picture very different from what you would expect. It talks of fighting, gambling and drinking being commonplace in the nave, and the only time a priest was seen was when he appeared on the rood loft to tell the crowd to keep quiet.

Old wooden lock box, Arlington

By the fourteenth century the division between priest and people, although still very obvious, was diminishing and pulpits were being installed for proper

The chancel arch at Friston

preaching instead of occasional short speeches from the rood loft. The pulpits were almost always three-decker affairs, consisting of a parish clerk's desk, the priest's reading desk and the preaching pulpit.

Almost all the three-deckers in Sussex have gone, although many survive in a cut down version. So many pulpits were installed in the seventeenth century that few were needed in the eighteenth; Northiam and Chiddingly are exceptions.

In the seventeenth century sermons become the norm, necessitating longer stays in church, and so pews appeared along with the majority of

The font at Berwick

pulpits. Box pews were the order of the day, much revered today but unbelievably uncomfortable, especially as early sermons often lasted two hours or more. Private pews for the local gentry, often very comfortable, started to appear along with the nave pews. Some contain fireplaces and ornate ceilings and almost all are set higher than the congregation, and even the priest. Warbleton's church has a fine example. Being privately owned, many of these pews have survived.

After the Reformation the separation between priest and people was reduced even more when the rood screens separating the chancel and nave were systematically removed. Although parts of some remain as parclose screens (Eastbourne) and reredos (Ovingdean), only a very few remain in situ.

The Dacre monument at Herstmonceux

Penhurst has a fine example. The rood beam was lost at the same time. This beam, where a cross (rood means cross) stood along with statues of the Virgin, St John and perhaps the church's patron saint, was an essential part of the medieval church. There are some modern ones giving an idea of what they were like. Bexhill has a nice one, but very few ancient ones remain. The stump of one can be seen jutting from the wall at Southease where it was sawn off; and many churches retain the stone corbels that supported them.

The rood loft was an extension of the beam and was sometimes large enough to contain an altar. The piscina that served the loft altar at Eastbourne can still be seen high up in the north wall. Fragments of the staircases that led to the lofts survive in many Sussex churches. There is a modern loft at Westham. The first preaching to the congregation was probably done from the rood loft.

A recent survey showed that fonts are the features that most church visitors come to see. The font is often the oldest thing in the church, and the only remaining item from the original building. Sussex has more than its share of ancient Norman ones along with some unusual and interesting

The font at Piddinghoe

later examples. At Udimore the font is made of wood and at Ashburnham the font is quite small and made of marble. At Berwick the font may be of Saxon origin and is built into the wall, while at Beddingham the font has hundreds of small crosses carved on it by happy parents over the years. Fonts installed from the sixteenth century onwards are much smaller, as total immersion was no longer the fashion. They are almost always near doors — a door was always left open during a christening to allow the Devil to depart.

At the other end of the nave squints (or hagioscopes) can often be found. These large angled portals cut through the wall between the nave and chancel allowed a priest performing the mass at a side altar in the nave or chapel to follow the service being performed at the main altar in the chancel. Hamsey and Guestling have fine examples. Almost all ancient churches contain at least one piscina, where the mass vessels were washed, many have a sedile, where the priest sat during parts of the service, and some have holy water stoups for use when entering or leaving the church and aumbrys where the mass vessels were kept.

A surprising number of churches still contain their ancient parish chests, usually a hollowed out tree trunk with a heavy lid banded with iron and containing three locks, one for each churchwarden and one for the priest.

RYE *St Mary the Virgin* OS🏛️93🍁🍁 ☆☆

he present church was started in the early twelfth century to replace the earlier wooden churches that had proved easy prey to the regular French raids. Even the stone building was not strong enough to resist the French raid of the town in 1377, when the roof and much of the nave were destroyed. The present nave arches were rebuilt at this time and reflect the style of the late fourteenth century. The church bells were stolen during this raid but recovered from France in a retaliation raid a year later.

The church is the largest parish church in the county and as early as 1522 was used to stage religious plays in front of large audiences. It is entered from the north transept and the visitor is faced with the fabulous south transept window as a first view of the inside. The church is filled with fine glass, none better than that in the north aisle by Burne-Jones, for my money his best window anywhere. The clock is one of the oldest church tower clocks still working and was made in 1561. The pendulum is 18ft long and hangs down into the nave at the crossing; the present clock face was made in 1760.

In the churchyard is a water tower built in 1736 at which time the vicar was paid seven shillings for the damage caused by digging the reservoir. A stone marks the spot where the mayor was chosen each year from 1289 to 1602. Two interesting graves are to be found next to each other; Allen Grebell was mistakenly murdered in the churchyard by John Breeds in 1742 and now they are lying next to each other. The flying buttresses are interesting; one dates from the fifteenth century and takes the strain from the arcades added at that time.

GUESTLING *St Laurence* OSSA 116   🏛 🏛 🍁 ☆

The church stands on high open ground with only a farm for company. It was built in the eleventh century as a simple two-cell church, and a tower was added in about 1100 — almost certainly for defence, as it had no door to the outside world; the tower doorway we see today is much later. The tower has a tall steep cap and an interesting clasping turret on its north-west side containing a newel stairway.

The chancel was rebuilt in the thirteenth century and now has buttresses at its eastern corners. The windows are for the most part lancets and quite plain. There is a particularly nice twelfth century chapel to the northeast with a fine entrance with deeply cut stone.

Following a bad fire in 1890 a great deal of the church interior was replaced, including a lot of the stonework, and this gives the inside a modern look — this applies particularly to the squint in the thirteenth century south chapel. There is evidence that one of the chapels was a chantry for a time.

The churchyard contains about a dozen very old, short, heavy headstones with a stylised skull as part of the decoration, all in the same area.

ICKLESHAM *All Saints with St Nicolas* OSSA 117 🏛🏛🏛 ❦❦ ☆☆☆

A place of worship has been recorded here since 772AD and the dedication, All Saints, was a Saxon favourite and may predate the present church — which is itself very old, being eleventh century with some additions between the twelfth and fourteenth centuries.

Entering through the unusual hexagonal west porch the immediate impression is of an almost totally early Norman church, with its rounded arches on massive pillars. The aisies add to the effect as they are not the normal fourteenth century additions but Norman originals; the south aisle even retains its twelfth century windows.

The three-stage tower has a particularly nice vaulted stone roof dated at about 1200. The dimensions of the church are also uncommon, the chancel (rebuilt thirteenth century) is longer than the nave and the bright airy St Nicolas chapel to the south is also very large. The nineteenth century restoration was carried out early in the century before the Victorian ideas of mass destruction took hold, and actually adds much to the church. The east window and spectacular font are from this time. The St Nicolas chapel seems to have been built at the same time as the rebuilding of the chancel and contains an interesting blind arcade containing stone shafts probably re-used from the original chancel.

The benefaction boards are considered the best in Sussex. These record gifts to the poor, such as land and rents, and give an insight into medieval life. This church in its pleasant setting is one not to be missed.

110

WINCHELSEA *St Thomas* OSSA 117

It is immediately obvious that this church was once very much larger, for the ruins of the original building form part of the present one. The church was built around 1300 when the town moved to this area following the destruction of the old town by the sea. Only sixty years later the priory-sized church was mostly destroyed by French raiders who sacked the town. It was never rebuilt but the remaining parts were restored and form the church we see today.

The churchyard is quite plain with few stones of interest; there are two military markers near the boundary wall. The effect on entering the church can be described only as breathtaking; the transformation from parish church to 'cathedral' is stunning.

On the north side are three effigies, probably from the church in the old town, a knight, a woman and a cleric. For anyone interested in twelfth century dress these are perfect examples. On the south side are three more from the fourteenth century, all of the Alard family. These are set in canopied tombs and beautifully lit.

The windows are massive and contain mostly twentieth century glass, although a little medieval glass can be seen in the north chancel. The arcade pillars are of Caen stone and Sussex marble and are a reminder of the building's former glory. The organ must get a mention for it is surely the biggest in Sussex. Set above the entrance (which has been reinforced to take the weight) it dominates the west wall.

111

WESTFIELD *St John the Baptist* OSSA 114

estfield is a beautifully proportioned church, even allowing for the large number of buttresses that seem to cover almost every surface. The clasping buttresses on the west corners of the tower fit in particularly well, making a short sturdy tower look even stronger.

The nave, chancel and tower are all twelfth century Through the south porch is the main door, dated 1542, and looking like it might serve another 500 years. The wooden lock box on its inside is a remarkable piece of work.

The church retains its original 800-year-old Norman chancel arch, slightly flattened on the top with the weight of the walls and with a squint on both sides. The lancet windows in the chancel are thirteenth century and date from the extending of the chancel to the east, but the actual east wall and window are later replacements. The ceiling of the chancel is highly painted, much as it would have been in medieval times. The north wall was lost when the nineteenth century aisle was built. This contains a large and very fine round stained glass window, which shouldn't suit this ancient church but somehow does. It's easy to miss the fourteenth century font, as its seventeenth century cover is so large it dominates the font, making it look like a truncated pillar. In fact the cover is so heavy that it needs a pulley system with a counterweight to raise it.

The churchyard is large and drops down to the southwest where most of the stones are. It contains a rare, seemingly un-restored wooden grave board dated 1916.

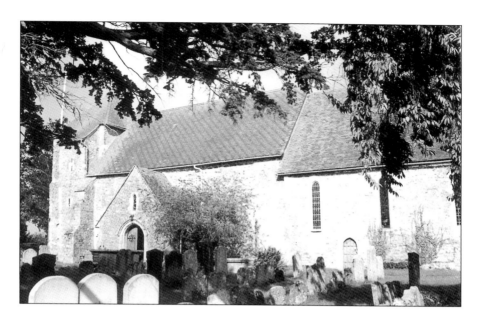

UDIMORE *St Mary* OSSA 91

The Domesday Book records a church at Udimore and part, if not all, of the nave may date from that time. There remains one Norman window (now blocked) in the north wall. The nave was enlarged at some time by adding a south aisle, which was later removed, returning the nave wall to its original position with the arches still visible.

The chancel and very low tower were added about 1230 . So low is the tower that if you were to take off its unusual overlapping cap it wouldn't even reach the nave roof apex. The modern south porch protects a fifteenth century doorway and window.

The chancel arch corbels have a rather nice, typically Norman, dog-tooth decoration, which is plain and simple like the rest of the building. The chancel is virtually unchanged since it was built and retains all six of its north and south lancet windows. The most westerly on the south side was lengthened to form a very long low side window (a technique often used in Sussex), but at a later date it was restored to its original size. The small priest's doorway is of a very plain design and none the worse for it.

The church has one feature unique in Sussex, a wooden font. Now replaced by a modern stone one the original is on display near the porch. It was made in the eighteenth century and painted to look like stone.

Most of the stones in the churchyard are to the south, as is often the case, and some are very old. Udimore's parish has always been a rural rather than a village one and its simple straightforward lines suit its purpose very well.

IDEN *All Saints* OSSA 70 🏛 ☆

Iden is one of those churches that have changed size over the years as needs dictate. Parts of the original small twelfth century church can still be seen but you really have to look for it as the building was at first considerably enlarged with the addition of aisles, then reduced by removing the south aisle.

The chancel was rebuilt in the thirteenth century as was the tower, which has also had a stair turret added. The blocked south arcade can clearly be seen both inside and out as part of the south wall but the blocked priest's door is only visible from the outside. The unusual square central pillar has a holy water stoup in its north face.

Many stones in the churchyard underline the closeness to the Kent border; a grotesque style is often found in that county, featuring coffins, skeletons and the tools of the grave digger. At Iden there is one military marker from the Second World War, for a soldier who died in Egypt in 1942.

SEDLESCOMBE *St John the Baptist* OSSA 88

In 1087 Domesday recorded an 'ecclesiola' or 'small church', which was probably of wood. Nothing remains of this building or its Norman replacement, the last vestiges of which disappeared in the nineteenth century when the thirteenth century chancel arch was removed. The tower, tower arch and nave roof are all fifteenth century The roof, with its king post, tie beams and wall plates, is of particular interest.

Both font and cover date from about 1600; the cover is a fine work of art. When made, it opened at the front to allow access to the font but now it is fixed to help preserve this ancient piece of woodwork. There are funeral hatchments mounted on the wall and the helmet above the door is also funeral apparel; these were made about three quarter size and placed on the coffin during the funeral.

The six bells are probably unique in that they date from 1595 to 1929, yet were all made at the same foundry in Whitechapel. The east window of the chancel is old and was reset in the new east wall in the nineteenth century, when the clear glass was replaced by the current stained glass. The glass is a memorial to John Pratt who was rector here for fifty-eight years.

There are many reasons why churches are often a long way from their village; this one was built in the middle of the parish rather than the middle of the village. The dedication is probably original as the church was in the hands of the Knights Hospitalers in the thirteenth century; their patron was John the Baptist.

SALEHURST *St Mary the Virgin* OSSA 64   🏛🏛 ☆☆

As we get nearer to the Kent border many of the churches become more imposing and less quaint, reflecting perhaps the wealth and denser population of this area in the past due to the iron industry. Salehurst is one of these, a huge church of Hastings sandstone which, at one time, catered for a much larger parish than it does now.

The tower is particularly massive, yet has no solid support walls inside the church; it stands on four huge pillars. There is a fine fourteenth century porch similar to that at Mountfield, but a later large stone porch to the west, with a vaulted roof, is more in keeping with the large church.

The nave is long with arcades; the roof and upper parts were replaced in the nineteenth century. The Norman font is interesting as it is believed to have been presented to the church by Richard I.

The churchyard is very large and quite unkempt. There are many very old stones and a couple of Harmer terracotta plaques can be seen. There are two military markers (Royal Artillery) and a very interesting 1920s deco style tomb for the Maxes Family. Viscountess Millner, daughter of Admiral Maxes, is buried here.

BODIAM *St Giles* OSSA 46

$\mathfrak{I}$n contrast to the nearby bold, prominent castle, the church at Bodiam is as hidden and inaccessible as any in the county. Perched on a wooded hill north of the castle it almost hangs over the deep cut road and access is via the narrowest of tracks (signposted Court Lodge Farm).

Although small it is of almost perfect dimensions and very pleasing to the eye. The tower is rare in that it is oblong, the widest side being north to south, and this seems to add to the feeling that the building is the right shape.

The church is mostly fourteenth century and many of the blocks are the same as those used in the castle, built 1385. Evidence below the now blocked priest's door hints at an earlier structure.

Extensively restored in 1851, the interior contains little from medieval times, just the chancel arch, some lancet windows, some fragments of brasses (one possibly fourteenth century) and the piscina and sedilia. The font is nineteenth century and has a huge counterbalanced cover.

The churchyard is small and contains the ever-present yew tree and some eighteenth century gravestones in a style more at home in nearby Kent than Sussex.

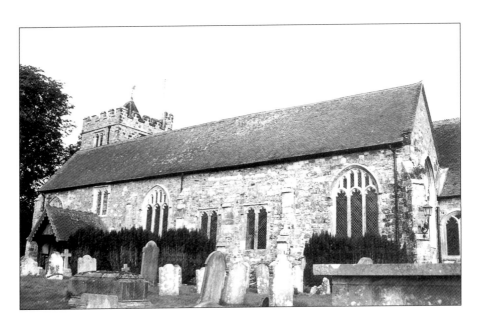

BREDE *St George* OSSA 90 🏛 ☆☆

𝕴n Norman times Brede would have been an important village standing as it does close to the River Brede, which was still navigable to the sea at that time.

As with many churches in villages that were busy or important, Brede's church has had many additions and changes over the years, and is a good example of many styles. In the twelfth century the south aisle was added to an existing nave which almost totally disappeared 100 years later when the building of the north aisle meant the removal of its remaining wall.

The tower was built in the fifteenth century at the same time as the Perpendicular style chancel, which is a little further east than its predecessor. The remaining western responds of the fourteenth century arches show where the original chapels stood before the chancel was moved. The present chapel is early sixteenth century and contains a particularly good example of a tomb chest. It is that of Sir Goddard Oxenbridge (d1537) and is complete with his effigy in Caen stone.

The nearby east window has much more elaborate tracery than is usual in England, and is more European in style. The font is also fifteenth century and retains some of its painted decoration. Nearby is an old poor box dated 1687.

The north porch is another addition and looks out on to a churchyard containing some interesting tombs and a few old stones. On the south side of the church roof is what must surely be one of the most unusual memorials in the county; it takes the form of an inscribed rain gutter, dated 1665.

118

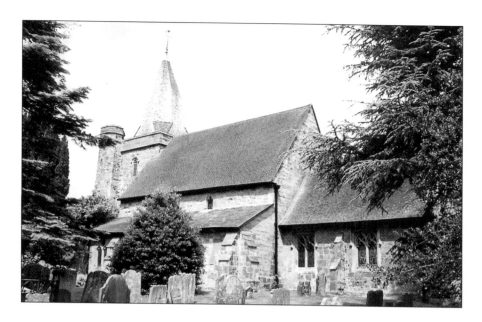

EWHURST *St James* OSSA 65 🏛 🍁🍁

Little remains of the original twelfth century church as most of what we see today is the result of either rebuilding or additions in the fourteenth century. At this time the nave roof was raised, making it much higher than the chancel (rebuilt at the same time), the tower was added to and its stair turret built on.

The spire is an odd shape, with the bottom half being steeper than the top and from some vantage points it appears to be twisted, but is not.

Inside the building the north arcade is interesting, incorporating part of the twelfth century church at its eastern end and a large corbel in the shape of a face at the western end. The south arcade is much plainer and from the Transitional period with typical round arches, but its simplicity is very pleasing to the eye. The thirteenth century font is made of Sussex marble.

The churchyard is famous for the unusual carving of the resurrection on one of its stones close to the tower, and for its extensive views. From here it is possible to see both the river Rother and the castle at Bodiam beyond.

BECKLEY *All Saints* OSSA 68 🏛 ⭐⭐

The church at Beckley sits up high on a mound and may stand on the site of a Saxon church. The present building has grown over the years, the oldest part is the lower stage of the tower which dates to about 1100. In the thirteenth century the south aisle was added and within 100 years the chancel was rebuilt, the north aisle inserted, the tower enlarged and the spire set in place. Much of the building was restored in the 1850s when the south chapel was added.

Entering the church it is necessary to descend a few steps to the floor level; this is quite rare. Inside the church is quite plain. Of interest are the high doorway, the remains of a stairway to a former rood loft and carvings in the form of that favourite Sussex pre-Christian belief, the Green Man.

The font is eighteenth century but part of the old Norman font is still on display. There is a fine example of an ancient dugout church chest with original metal banding and three locks.

The churchyard is large but not overpopulated; there is one military marker for an air force pilot from the Second World War, a sad reminder that much of the Battle of Britain was fought in the sky above Sussex and Kent.

NORTHIAM *St Mary*

OSSA 67 🏛 ☆☆

orthiam is a village close to the Kent border and its church has the harder, more austere look of that county. The ironstone construction and one of the three remaining ancient stone spires in Sussex may contribute to this feeling. The lower bulk of the tower is all that remains of the twelfth century church, the original nave walls having disappeared in the fourteenth century when the aisles and south porch were added.

Another common addition in this part of the county, the stair turret, does nothing to enhance the look of the building. Apart from the tower the other dominant feature is the huge mausoleum built on to the north side of the church. It is perhaps the most impressive in Sussex, and contains the tombs of, and is adorned with the shields of, the Frewen family, residents of the town for more than 400 years.

Inside the church several old ledger slabs are set in the floor and there are two brasses from the 1500s. Three items from the eighteenth century, a period from which little church furnishing remains, are preserved — the royal arms of Queen Anne (1713), a brass chandelier (1727) and a rare pulpit, one of only two or three remaining in Sussex.

There is a small horse drawn hearse on show and some items from the earlier chancel given to the church by the aptly named Thankful Frewen in 1638.

PEASMARSH *St Peter and St Paul* OSSA 68 🏛🏛 ✰✰

There was certainly a church at Peasmarsh before the conquest, but the oldest parts of the present, picturesquely sited building, date from about 1070. Parts of the nave walls and the chancel arch are of this date and the almost unaltered chancel arch is perhaps the church's best feature. The interesting carvings of wild animals to be seen either side of the arch are contemporary, and there were certainly many more of these. Some still survive both inside and out, although these others have probably been re-positioned.

The tower was added about 1170 and is rare in that its design is neither Norman nor Early English, but of a sub-period called the Trans-Norman. The aisles were added at the same time as the tower by knocking away most of the existing walls and inserting arches, also in the Trans-Norman style. When the chancel was enlarged in the early thirteenth century a low side window was added. This was clearly unglazed, as the marks of three bars and the remains of a shutter latch can still be seen. The position of the rood loft is clear from the entrance still visible high in the wall. The commandments, Lord's Prayer and creed above the chancel arch are painted on plaster board and date from the time of Elizabeth I. This is called a triptych and would have formed part of something larger and in a different part of the church originally.

The vertical belfry ladder is an unusual and dangerous looking item that I wouldn't like to try out.The churchyard has some interesting stones including two military, both for soldiers in the Royal Artillery.

PLAYDEN *St Michael* OSSA 93 🏛🏛 🍁 ☆☆

his almost unaltered twelfth century church is built to the 'axial tower plan', an unusual format where the tower is enclosed by the nave and chancel and stands between the two. The only other one in Sussex that springs to mind is at North Lancing in West Sussex. The roof extends very low on both sides but this is a later addition, for there is evidence of an earlier clerestory in the form of two windows visible from inside the church above the arcades. All the windows are replacements with the exception of an original Norman round-headed one in the north aisle.

The Transitional style is much in evidence inside the church where the arcade pillars alternate between round and octagonal. There is here a good example of architectural needs causing the changes between the Norman and the Early English styles. The tower arches are Early English pointed type which could stand the greater weight of the tower, while the arcades, although slightly later, are of the rounded Norman style still in fashion at that time.

The small plain chancel was partly rebuilt in the sixteenth century and the east window is of that date. The parclose screen under the north tower arch is extremely rare thirteenth century work and very finely carved. The east arch screen is fifteenth century and offers another comparison of changing styles. Not so delicately made but of great interest is the massive belfry ladder, dated 1686 but now thought to be much older.

The most interesting memorial inside is that of a brewer with the tools of his trade carved into the stone; the inscription is in Flemish.

EAST GULDEFORD *St Mary* OSSA 93

f you are looking for a church that looks a little different then this is it. Built in 1505 on reclaimed land, it has to be said that it looks a little like a double roofed barn with a bell turret in the middle. It was built by Sir Robert Guldeford, entirely of brick, and stands just a mile or so from the Kent border.

Few churches were built at this time and the design may reflect a more Puritan ideal. Inside the church the rectangular shape is repeated with just a decorated roof timber to mark the nave from the chancel. There are some nice box pews and an unusual two-level pulpit, both from the end of the eighteenth century. The font is much older (twelfth century) and must have come from another church.

Parking is difficult and a walk along a narrow path is needed to reach the church. In common with many Sussex churches sheep are often left to graze in the churchyard to keep the grass down

ISFIELD *St Margaret* OSSA 102 ☆

Originally both village and church stood together on the river Uck close to where it joins the Ouse, but when the village moved (perhaps the importance of the river diminished, or that common medieval cloud, the plague, descended on the area) the church was left in stately isolation. It is reached via the narrowest of lanes, but a sizeable parking exists. A huge and very ancient oak shrouds the front and it is necessary to walk round to the north side where the churchyard is at its widest to get a full view of the building.

The south wall is thirteenth century, and although there was an older tower the lower part of this one dates from the fifteenth century. The top portion of the tower and its central spire are Victorian but the spire adds nothing to the look of the building as a whole. There is a large grave plot for the King family and a very old grave slab is built into the nave wall.

Inside the church the Decorated period prevails to the east and south and the east window is particularly good. The squint between the south chapel and the chancel demonstrates its original use very well allowing a priest at the chapel altar to follow the mass at the main altar. Evidence of the original tower can be found in the late twelfth century tower arch, which is also the oldest feature.

There are some fine sixteenth century memorials in the south chapel to the Shurley family, who adopted the chapel in the 1500s. The oldest is dated 1527 and the largest (Sir John, his wife and nine children portrayed in alabaster) dated 1631. It may well have been these patrons who added the interesting poppy-headed benches which date from this time.

CHIDDINGLY OSSA 105 🏛🏛 ☆☆

Of the three remaining ancient stone spires in Sussex, Chiddingly is the oldest. Perched on the Perpendicular Pelham tower and surrounded by four pinnacles, it does little to improve the looks of the church, which from some directions appear very stark.

The building dates from about 1260, with the nave arcades being added about 100 years later. These give on to aisles the west end of which retain some early lancet windows. Some interesting old box pews remain along with some large seventeenth and eighteenth century ledger slabs which are set into the floor of the nave and chancel. The chancel was rebuilt in the nineteenth century. In the south transept there is a large alabaster memorial to Sir John Jefferay (d1578), which is considered one of the best in the country and which has recently been beautifully restored to much of its former glory. Other smaller tablets and plaques to the Jefferay family, who built the nearby manor, adorn the walls.

The Pelham family's buckle badge is in evidence, forming label stops on the tower's west doorway. Close to that most popular of later positions for the church entrance, the north porch, a gravestone retains a Harmer terracotta plaque. One wooden graveboard remains in the churchyard but although in its original position it is a modern copy.

The church carries no dedication today although Chiddingly was the home of a minor Saxon saint.

EAST HOATHLY OSSA 105 ☆☆

he oldest surviving part of the church is the fifteenth century 'Pelham' tower. The family seat was originally at nearby Laughton and the Pelhams were great church benefactors, especially when it came to towers. Many churches in this part of East Sussex have a Pelham tower distinguishable by its typical fifteenth century Perpendicular style and the addition of the Pelham buckle, the family badge, which can usually be found as label stops, or the like. This tower is short, with a stair turret rising slightly higher than the tower's battlements. Inside, the tower arch is very tall and has interesting responds and capitals.

The rest of the church was rebuilt in the nineteenth century; the tower probably survived only because of its Pelham background. There is a hint of a very much older church on the site in a very rare Norman piscina mounted on an original short Norman pillar, decorated with a typical early Norman chevron design. This type of piscina is the forerunner of the more common wall niche type.

One or two small memorials survive from before the rebuilding but very little else. The churchyard contains some early eighteenth century stones including one to the Sussex diarist, Thomas Turner, who lived in the village. There is at least one Harmer terracotta to be found.

The tower boasts a nice clock and full peal of bells.

FLETCHING *St Andrew and St Mary the Virgin* OSSA 85 🍁 ☆☆☆

This is a fine example of an early English style cruciform church. It is said that the lower part of the tower is Saxon but this is unlikely as the Domesday Book lists no church here, and such an mistake would have been rare. The church sits up high in a huge churchyard that stretches away behind the church. The porch is fifteenth century and like the church is roofed with Horsham stone slabs. The door, although restored, is 500 years old, so as you enter it is worth a thought that this is the same door people opened in Henry VIII's time. The chancel is wider than the nave, which is very rare and hints at a link with an abbey or monastery. The east window looks to have been a thirteenth century architectural experiment and is like no other.

Edward Gibbon author of *The Decline and Fall of the Roman Empire,* is interred in the Earl of Sheffield's mausoleum, and Simon de Montfort sat an all night vigil here before the battle of Lewes in 1264. The following day he defeated the King and sowed the seeds of England's parliamentary government system.

There are too many interesting monuments to mention them all, but two are of particular interest — a simple brass of two gloves for a glover who joined Jack Cade in his revolt against the crown in the early fifteenth century, and the beautiful marble effigies of Richard Leche, High Sheriff of Sussex and Surrey, and his wife. The wife remarried after Richards's death but her second husband was so unkind to her she had her effigy placed next to Richard's while she still lived. The small skull between them indicates the death of their child.

LITTLE HORSTED *St Michael and All Angels* OSSA 78

Horsted is a Saxon word meaning horse station and there has probably been a church on this site since the earliest times of this village. In fact the arcade of four blocked windows in the Norman chancel may well be of Saxon origin although the Norman style windows cut into two of them are modern.

The tower is dated 1450 but the turret was added during the extensive rebuilding undertaken by Sir Gilbert Scott in 1863. The oldest of the six bells was made about 1530 and is dedicated to St Catherine, whose cult flourished in England during the middle ages with 170 medieval bells still bearing her name today.

Inside, almost hidden by the choir stalls, is a tomb recess containing a tapering coffin slab with a raised cross dated 1502. Also of interest is an eighteenth century statue of the Virgin Mary.

In common with many Sussex churches the north porch is a recent addition and the much older west door is of more interest with its carvings of a Tudor rose and that oldest of Sussex motifs the Green Man.

BUXTED *St Margaret the Queen* OSSA 56 🏛 🍁 ☆

Many churches stand alone as a result of the village having moved, but few for the same reason as Buxted. In 1830 the Lord of the manor relocated the village of Buxted to land outside the grounds of his manor to gain more privacy. The manor is now a hotel and the church stands alone in its park-like grounds.

The church, which carries the very rare dedication to St Margaret, Queen of Scots, is for the most part thirteenth century with much good restoration. The tower is a little later and has a broach spire containing eight bells. The churchyard is small with a nice boundary wall. The early English nave has four bay aisles to both north and south. The chancel is from the Decorated period and the plaster ceiling depicting hop branches comes as a bit of a surprise for a parish church, but is in near perfect condition.

The roof was probably raised in the seventeenth century when the clerestory windows were added; the very heavy communion rail is of the same date, as is the altar in the restored south chapel. The font and nearby carved chest are thirteenth century.

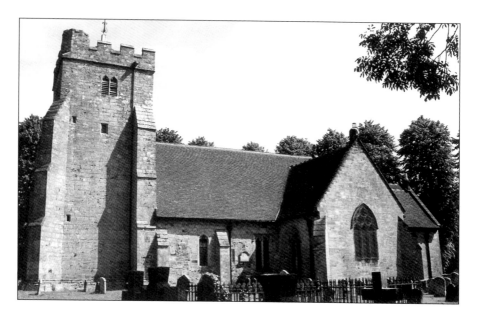

MARESFIELD *St Bartholomew* OSSA 55 ☆

The church was almost entirely rebuilt in the nineteenth century, with only the tower surviving from the fifteenth century. The tower's west door and window are original and the interior tower arch is noteworthy for its great height. A few other features of the medieval church are to be seen but all have been moved about and re-sited; these include a narrow Norman window in the south wall, the somewhat damaged font, the ancient chancel arch, which is now in the north transept, and the old east window which is now in the south.

Some old woodwork has survived, namely the eighteenth century pulpit and communion rail and the much older carved north doorframe. The royal arms are those of George I.

The churchyard is surrounded by trees and contains a number of early stone markers in the same shape as the now almost extinct wooden grave boards.

ROTHERFIELD *St Denys* OSSA 39

church on this site can be accurately traced back 1,200 years by its dedication, for it is known that a Saxon lord, Berhtwald, built a church here as an offering of thanks after being cured of an illness at the monastery of St Denys in France.

The present church is made up of eleventh, twelfth and thirteenth century parts with fifteenth century additions; the oldest parts are the nave, chancel and the Nevill chapel. This 900-year-old chapel has been much altered as blocked windows testify, and there was probably a similar chapel on the south side of the church at some time.

The wall paintings date between the thirteenth and fifteenth centuries and must have once covered every wall space, though some have faded since their uncovering in 1890. The Doom above the chancel arch is the most impressive.

The Norman font was lost for many years until found in a field some way south of the village and reinstated in the nineteenth century. The most interesting glass is the rare nineteenth century pre-Raphaelite example in the east window, designed by Edward Burne-Jones and made by William Morris.

There are several old memorials inside the church but none older than the unmarked iron grave slab just inside the north door. It is decorated with a cross and is thought to be as early as fourteenth century.

The stone porch has a small room above, said to have held an early school, but if this is true it has either been altered or the people were very short. The yew in the churchyard is at least 1,400 years old.

FRAMFIELD *St Thomas à Becket* OSSA 70

Following a major fire in 1509 the old church on this site was almost totally rebuilt, with only the thirteenth century north chapel, the remains of the rood loft stairway and possibly the squint surviving. At the time of the rebuilding this area was the major iron producing area in England and the rebuilt church reflects this prosperity. The main fabric of the church, the nave, clerestory, and south chapel are all from this rebuilding. Even the building materials reflect its iron industry background, for the sandstone blocks are veined with iron ore.

The tower collapsed in the mid-seventeenth century and was not replaced until the late nineteenth, at which time the chancel was again rebuilt.

The church contains a good number of fine memorials but all seem to date from the sixteenth century rebuilding to the present day. The glass in the south chapel is clear but very old and some may be original. The older glass is slightly cloudy and has a greenish hue.

The churchyard is large but sparsely populated with some old stones removed to the boundary wall. The north stone porch faces the village which butts up to the churchyard on that side. The dedication is to St Thomas à Becket and was probably not that of the early church. The Tudor rebuilding may have offered the chance to honour this saint who had connections with Sussex.

HARTFIELD *St Mary the Virgin* OSSA 13 🏛 🍁 ☆

St Mary's is well known for its lych gate, which is perhaps one of the most unusual in the country — being an integral part of an ancient half-timbered cottage.

The church stands on a near-treeless mound in a large, well-populated churchyard. From the thirteenth century there remains only the rough built north wall with one blocked lancet window. The south side of the building including the Decorated windows and chapel is fourteenth century. The Perpendicular west tower with shingled broach spire has fifteenth century windows and may be of that date.

Inside there is evidence of considerable rebuilding, although the date of this is unclear. The sixteenth century would be a good guess as it seems the rood loft, rood screen and chancel arch were removed during this rebuilding and a sixteenth century double tie-beam has taken their place. The oldest memorial is in the south chapel and is dated 1640; it takes the form of a wall tablet with long Latin inscription. There are a large number of other wall tablets, mostly nineteenth century. To the west is a large Perpendicular-style carved font.

WITHYHAM *St Michael and All Angels* OSSA 14

ithyham is interesting in that it is a rare example of a church built almost entirely in the seventeenth century The north nave wall and south chancel wall , together with the lower part of the tower, are all that remain of the earlier church, which was destroyed by lightning in 1663.

The current building was complete by 1680 when the huge Sackville chapel was added. Since then the only changes have been the addition of the south aisle and the removal of the north. The font (dated 1666) and five-light east window are both contemporary with the main structure.

The overwhelming feeling when entering the church is one of immense space emphasised by the unusual sandy-coloured block construction and the massive Sackville chapel, built directly north of the main altar and completely dwarfing the chancel. The chapel contains many family memorials but all are overshadowed by the large altar tomb by Cibber, depicting the thirteen-year-old Thomas Sackville flanked by the life-size kneeling figures of his parents. The chapel also contains a plaque to author and poet Vita Sackville West (d1962). In all the church has a nice, bright, airy feeling.

THE TOP TEN

These are the ten churches that score highest, using my rating system — for historical interest, architectural interest and picturesque setting.

Icklesham: Something for everyone here, just fails a perfect score on its setting.
Winchelsea: Joint number one with a matching score, a stunner in every way.
Mountfield: Much of interest here including extensive views.
Piddinghoe: One for the architecture fans with plenty of history too.
Penhurst: Take your camera, the setting is second to none.
Withyham: The very floors are covered with Sussex history.
Bishopstone: A must for everyone's touring list.
Arlington: Historical interest everywhere.
Alfriston: This unique church has to feature.
Berwick: Fair on the outside, one of a kind on the inside.

Close behind come **Rodmell, Etchingham, Southease, Catsfield** and **Rye.**

Canopy-side tombs at Winchelsea

136

THE PATRON SAINTS OF EAST SUSSEX CHURCHES

All Saints: All the known and unknown Christian martyrs (possibly a dedication of Saxon origin).

St Andrew: Apostle preached in Near East after Christ's death, believed to have been crucified at Patras in Achaia and his body recovered by crusaders in 1204 and returned to Italy. Also thought to have travelled to Scotland and built a church in Fife. Patron saint of Scotland and fishermen.

St Anne: Mother of the Virgin Mary, usually depicted teaching the Virgin to read.

St Bartholomew: First century scholar who preached Christianity in India and Armenia. Said to have been executed at Derbend on the Caspian Sea. Remains eventually returned to Italy. Patron saint of tanners.

St Clement: First century bishop of Rome exiled to the Crimea where he was killed by having an anchor chain wrapped round him and being thrown into the sea. Patron saint of lighthousemen.

Sts Cosmos and Damian: Twins who became doctors and Christians, practicing their profession without taking payment from their patients. Both were martyred at Cyrrhus. Patron saints of doctors and pharmacists.

St Denys: Third century bishop of Paris, Italian-born he travelled to Gaul to convert and build a church on an island in Paris. He was killed there and thrown into the river. An abbey was built on the spot where his body was recovered.

St Dunstan: Tenth century Archbishop of Canterbury, of noble birth, was educated at Glastonbury. Twice exiled from court, he rose to become leader of the English church. Died 988. Patron saint of the blind, blacksmiths and goldsmiths.

St George: Replaced Edward the Confessor as patron saint of England after the crusades. Thought to be a soldier who died in Palestine under the persecution of the Christians by Diocletian around 303AD. Patron saint of soldiers, archers and knights.

St Giles: Eighth century hermit who founded a monastery in France, which became a stopping place for pilgrims travelling to the Holy Land. Returning crusaders spread his cult. Patron saint of cripples, lepers, hermits and mothers.

St James: One of Christ's apostles, executed in 44AD by Herod Agrippa. Preached in Spain. Was adopted by crusaders as defender of the faith. Patron saint of pilgrims.

St John the Baptist: John's mother was cousin to the Virgin Mary. He began preaching before Christ, and baptized Christ. Made an enemy of Herod Antipas and his wife who demanded his head for comments he had made. Was arrested and killed without trial.

St Jude: First century apostle who joined with St Simon and preached in Persia, where both were martyred. Patron saint of lost causes.

St Laurence: Third century deacon of Rome executed under the persecution of Valerian in 258AD. Recorded his own acts in writing, which his cult follows. Patron saint of deacons, firefighters and cooks.

St Leonard: Sixth century hermit, who started life as a nobleman, founded an abbey at Noblac, where he died and is buried.

St Margaret of England: A Cistercian nun, who travelled to the Holy Land, settled in Sauve Benite where she died. Patron saint of dying.

St Margaret of Scotland: Daughter of Edward the Atheling who fled to Scotland after the Norman Conquest. Revived the church in Scotland and built churches and hostels there. Devoted her life to others and died in 1093.

St Margaret of Antioch: Probably a fictitious character whose cult was spread by returning crusaders. Said to be the daughter of a pagan priest, she was executed for her Christian beliefs. Patron saint of childbearing.

St Martin: Born in Hungary, the son of a pagan army officer, joined the army but was discharged for his Christian beliefs, stayed on in France where he worked against paganism. Buried at Tours. Patron saint of beggars and soldiers.

St Mary: The Blessed Virgin, mother of Christ. After the death of Christ went to Turkey under the protection of St John where she lived out her life. Patron saint of mothers, nuns, and virgins.

St Mary Magdalene: Follower of Christ. Thought to be a sinner. Witnessed the resurrection. Perhaps a true apostle but this fact may have been suppressed during the early times of the Christian religion when the role of women was unsure. Patron saint of women's hairdressers, penitents, and prostitutes.

St Matthew: Former tax collector, who joined the apostles and wrote the first gospel. Patron saint of bankers, accountants and taxmen.

St Michael: The archangel, messenger and defender of God, his cult usually associated with churches on high ground. Patron saint of radiologists and the sick.

St Nicholas: Bishop of Myra in present day Turkey, his remains were brought to Italy in the eleventh century, at which time his cult spread throughout Europe. Most famous as Santa Claus, probably due to his custom of giving dowries to poor women on their wedding day, and his patronage of children. Patron saint of children, Russia, sailors and pawnbrokers.

St Oswald: Soldier king of Northumbria who became a Christian in Iona. Killed and mutilated by a pagan king at the battle of Maserfield and his body parts buried in various places causing his cult to spring up over a wide area. Patron saint of soldiers.

St Pancras: An orphan brought to Rome where he was converted only to be martyred at the age of fourteen. His cult arrived in England in 664 when the Pope sent relics of the saint to King Oswiu, king of Northumbria.

St Paul: Nobleman who was converted to Christianity after a vision. Tirelessly tried to spread Christianity until his beheading in Rome at the time of Nero; he was buried outside the walls of Rome.

St Peter: Leader of the apostles, who preached mostly in Rome. Crucified by Nero possibly at the same time as St Paul as they both share the same saint's day and are often linked together. Patron saint of fishermen.

St Sithe/St Zita: Roman serving girl who gave her master's food to the poor and came to grief because of it. Patron saint of housewives.

St Thomas à Becket: Archbishop of Canterbury who was killed at his own altar after political differences with the then king of England, Henry II, who was made to do public penance by the Pope.

St Wulfran/St Wulfram: Seventh century monk and missionary from France who converted heathen tribes to Christianity with varying degrees of success. Only two churches are dedicated to him in this country.

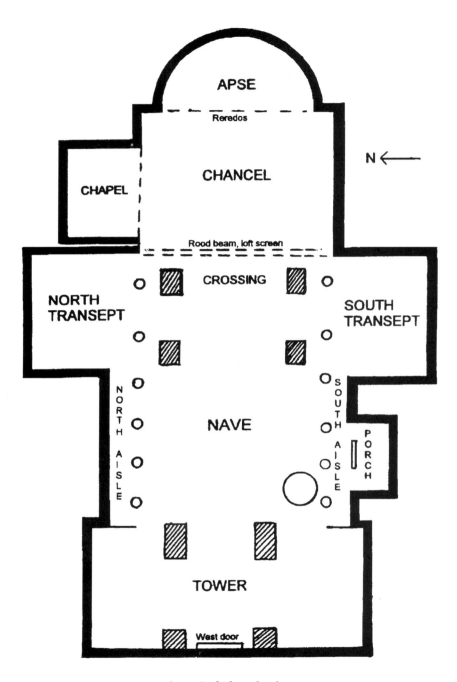

APSE

Reredos

CHANCEL

CHAPEL

Rood beam, loft screen

CROSSING

NORTH
TRANSEPT

SOUTH
TRANSEPT

N O R T H · A I S L E

NAVE

S O U T H · A I S L E

P O R C H

TOWER

West door

N ←

A typical church plan

A RECOMMENDED 2¹/₂ HOUR TOUR FOR EACH AREA

BRIGHTON'S VILLAGES

Start at ancient Ovingdean with its crowded churchyard and solid squat tower, drive south to the coast and a mile east to well-kept Rottingdean, famous for its artistic parishioners both past and present. Return to the A259 coast road and drive east again, turning inland on the C7 at Newhaven. Turn left at the sign for Telscombe two miles north and enjoy the spectacular drive across the top of the downs to the picturesque and historic church.

THE LOWER OUSE

Start at Rodmell with its Bloomsbury group connections then travel south towards the sea. Next off to the left of the main road comes round-towered Southease. From there move on to another round tower at Piddinghoe; plenty of history here, so allow for a long stop. Keep going south to Newhaven, then cross the river and head towards Seaford. Turn left when you see the Bishopstone sign to visit the imposing part-Saxon church just a half-mile inland.

LEWES'S NORTHERN VILLAGES

Start near the county's western border at Ditchling, where the impressive cruciform church lies in the shadow of Ditchling Beacon. Then head east along the Lewes road to take in first, pretty Westmeston, and then sturdy Plumpton with its ancient wall paintings. Keep travelling east eventually taking a left turn marked East Chiltington to visit the secluded church there. For those who like a challenge, take the unmade road behind the church following the old Roman road direct to Streat church.

CUCKMERE VALLEY

Commence with the paintings in Berwick church then cut back across the A27 to historic Arlington, cross the A27 again to not-to-be-missed Alfriston. Continue south, climbing high over the downs towards the sea. Turn left at the A259, cross the river's meanders, then left again at Exceat to return up the other side of the valley. Visit unique West Dean and, if there's time, tiny Lullington.

EASTBOURNE AND ITS VILLAGES

Begin with a long look at St Mary's, Eastbourne, before moving inland on the A22 London road, taking in Willingdon, with its offset tower just before Polegate. At Polegate turn left on to the A27. To visit remote Folkington take the tiny lane on the left marked Folkington Lane, otherwise continue west to

Wilmington, which will come up on the left. Be sure to take a look at the ruined priory and pay your respects to the 1600-year-old yew tree and the prehistoric Long Man on the nearby hillside.

LOW WEALD AND PEVENSEY LEVELS
Westham and Pevensey cling to each side of Pevensey castle so start with these two. Then head inland from the A27 roundabout at Pevensey for a picturesque ride across the levels, eventually passing Wartling church. Next, go on up the hill to the main road at the top. Turn left towards Herstmonceux; the church with its famous Dacre tomb is off to the left before the village is reached.

1066 COUNTRY
There is a lot to see at Bexhill so start there. Then turn inland towards Ninfield taking in the church there. At Ninfield take the B2204 to Catsfield with its unique Holy Water stoup. On then to Battle before turning towards London to visit Jack Fuller's tomb at Brightling, and Mountfield which has something for everyone.

HIGH WEALD
The ancient stone spire at Dallington church is a good place to start, then north east to unchanged Etchingham. North again to majestic Ticehurst ending up near the Kent border at Wadhurst.

RYE AND THE EASTERN VILLAGES
The first choice tour (three hours minimum). Start with the tower at Rye church then leave the town on the A259 going west to Top Ten joint winner, breath-taking Winchelsea. Not far along the same road is the other number one, Icklesham. Two miles on find Guestling to the left with its ancient tower and Westfield to the right, a photographer's dream.

UCKFIELD AND ASHDOWN FOREST VILLAGES
Begin at Chiddingly with its stone spire and Jefferay memorial, then travel northwest to historic Fletching, taking in Newick on the way. Due east from there is Buxted in its parkland setting. Trek north through the forest to Withyham ending up at Hartfield with its unique lych gate.

ABOUT THE AUTHOR

Paul Coppin was born in South London in 1950. In 1965 he joined the family business, which he now runs. His interests have always been wide and varied; he was a semi-professional American football referee for thirteen years and is a keen collector of Goss heraldic china. He married his wife Janice in 1970 and they have one daughter. In 1999 Paul and Janice moved from London to a small hamlet just outside Lewes, where they now live.

S. B. Publications publish a wide range of local interest books on Sussex and other counties in England. For a free catalogue write to:-
S B Publications, 19 Grove Road, Seaford, East Sussex BN25 1TP
or access our website on:-
www.sbpublications.swinternet.co.uk